Jocassee
face of the waters

~

Jocassee
face of the waters

~

Poems
April Phillips Boone

Copyright © 2018 by April Phillips Boone

All rights reserved. No portion of this book may be reproduced in any form or by any means, including electronic storage and retrieval systems, except by explicit, prior written permission of the author, except for brief passages excerpted for review and critical purposes.

∼

Cover art and design: Rebekah Sather
Interior layout: April Phillips Boone

Boone, April Phillips.
Jocassee face of the waters : poems / April Phillips Boone.
ISBN 978-0692099759
April Phillips Boone, Publisher: Marshall, NC 28753
First printing 2018

Dedicated to

Adam David Worley

1978-2018

I had just finished writing this collection of poems when I heard that Adam Worley had passed from this life to the next in a kayaking accident. As one memorial to him states, Adam "began his final adventure to truly see God's face on New Year's Eve 2017". In Adam's last social media post, he uploaded a video from his location on the water, showing a sublimely beautiful sun that, in the process of setting, colored the waves all numbers of shades of brilliant white, silver and golden yellow, fiery orange, red, pink, and purple on shining water and sky. Included with the sunset video was this caption he had written: "And to think this happens at the end of every single day….get out and see it!!" So, I dedicate this work to Adam, for his sense of adventure and wonder, his love of nature, and his passion for the One who created and sustains it all. Because of these things, Adam's influence will continue to color the lives of those who remain, like the sunset on those rippling waves.

To Kevin Boone

Thank you, my love!!!

Contents

I. Introduction
1. Seeing Into the Life of Things ~ 3
2. Revelation of a Double Mind (including the poem *Prelude:* Double Mind) ~ 7
3. Reading Poetry: A Few Tips for Enjoyment and Understanding ~ 15

II. Poems:
Jocassee's Mine ~ 19
Mediator ~ 25
The Venture ~ 25
Austere Miles ~ 26
Destiny ~ 27
Tacking ~ 27
slow fin parts surface ~ 30
Deep ~ 30
a piece of pure lake ~ 32
Broken ~ 32
Not Drifting ~ 33
Water on the Line ~ 34
May Bees ~ 36
Cold Comfort ~ 37
Warm Marrow ~ 38
Palindrome Dreams ~ 39
Catch and Release ~ 40
Ease ~ 41
The Point ~ 42
Hardy ~ 43
eight-inch turtle head ~ 44
Toward Restitution ~ 44

Reach ~ 47
Finding Fault (Spiritual Tectonics) ~ 51
A Start ~ 53
now that the scales have fallen ~ 54
Living Water ~ 54
What's New? ~ 55
Welcome Home ~ 57
Water Proof ~ 59
Survival Course ~ 60
Hold Your Fire ~ 61
Blue Wall Psalms ~ 62
Wild Honey ~ 68
Jocassee's Green Bird ~ 69
Cosmic Storm ~ 70
Umbrella Sailing ~ 73
Wright Creek Bluegrass ~ 74
Variations on a Twinkle ~ 76
Eastern Phoebe at Horsepasture River ~ 77
Homeowners ~ 77
Shine ~ 78
Ancient Call ~ 80
Testify! ~ 81
water in the air ~ 86
Jumping Off Rock ~ 86
Carpe Diem ~ 87
Expanding Range ~ 88
Lift Up the Serpent ~ 90
Rattled (Rattlesnake Joe) ~ 91
Double Springs Harmonic ~ 93
Whistling: A Handbook ~ 95
Everything ~ 106
Mother of All Theories ~ 106
Precipitation 100% ~ 111
Ducks in a Row ~ 111

Trilocation ~ 112
Depth Perception Deception ~ 114
Fear Itself ~ 116
Things Angels Desire to Look Into ~ 121
Put Out the Night ~ 125

Notes ~ 135

About the Author ~ 157

I

Introduction

~

1. Seeing Into the Life of Things

These 62 poems are my labor of love for a mesmerizing place. My husband and I have kayaked many of Florida's blue, spring-fed rivers, with animated otters fishing next to our boats on Dunellon's sparkling Rainbow River, and with mostly lethargic but a few alert and hungry alligators on Ocala's Silver and Withlacoochie Rivers. We've floated with manatees in Homasassa and Crystal Rivers, and befriended raccoons, needlenose gar, and gentle manatees on the consistently turquoise Weeki Wachee River of Spring Hill. We've also paddled through elephant-seal-filled, harbor-seal-, humpback-whale-, killer-whale-filled waters off the San Juan Islands of Washington State, and the shark-riddled tidal river called Battery Creek in Beaufort, SC. Once, in Battery Creek, a pod of dolphins allowed me to kayak beside them and their babies, all of us in motion together until they outpaced me around the bend. Still, even with all these experiences, I find myself most enchanted by the first place where I fully experienced and understood the vitality of water and the life it supports: Lake Jocassee in Salem, South Carolina.

The first time I saw the lake, I was awestruck by its beauty. In the course of living, however, I forgot about the lake for years until I rediscovered it while taking a drive after a day of teaching in nearby Greenville County. I began to kayak there, and the lake became my spiritual haven and retreat, place of restoration through solitude, and place where I physically challenged myself (in day trips, sometimes as far as 18 miles) to kayak to see each of the waterfalls that spill into the lake, and all four of the rivers that tumble out of the mountains to feed the major part of its depths. In the process, I came to know the lake and its wild surroundings intimately: I saw and touched the face of the waters.

So, like a true Romantic, I come here chasing beauty. And I have had times of being purely overwhelmed by the beauty here – beauty of the laws of physics in my boat's motion across the stirred lake and in rapidly changing forces of the winds; beauty of light and its interplay with the beauty of water; beauty of beaches, islands, rocks and forest; and beauty in the biology of creatures who make this home.

In the late eighteenth and early nineteenth centuries, Romantic poets began a revolution in poetry in which, among other goals, they sought to capture nature in all her glory. However, for all these poets (including major Romantics Wordsworth, Coleridge, Shelley, Byron, and Keats), their poetic projects went beyond writing eloquent lines that froze nature's beauty on a page. Their larger objective was to use nature's beauty to make humankind better. Their belief was that by developing the awareness and the sense to see (and hear and touch) nature's exquisite beauty, a person would always be led to be more wise, more compassionate, more spiritually refined, and more in tune with a higher truth.

I agree, and I come to Jocassee for all those reasons. Through adventures on the water and quiet solitude observing nature's beauty, I have experienced serenity and a sharpening of vision. It's a state of being Wordsworth captures when he writes in "Tintern Abbey" of revisiting a favorite outdoor place on the banks of the Wye River:

> To them I may have owed another gift,
> Of aspect more sublime; that blessed mood,
> In which the burthen of the mystery,
> In which the heavy and the weary weight
> Of all this unintelligible world
> Is lighten'd:—that serene and blessed mood,
> In which the affections gently lead us on,
> Until, the breath of this corporeal frame,
> And even the motion of our human blood
> Almost suspended, we are laid asleep

> In body, and become a living soul:
> While with an eye made quiet by the power
> Of harmony, and the deep power of joy,
> We see into the life of things. (lines 37-50)

Also inspired by a watery place, Byron, in *Childe Harold's Pilgrimage*, depicts the ocean as reflecting God's face:

> Thou glorious mirror, where the Almighty's form
> Glasses itself in tempests; in all time,
> Calm or convuls'd—in breeze, or gale, or storm,
> Icing the pole, or in the torrid clime
> Dark-heaving;—boundless, endless, and
>   sublime—
> The image of Eternity—the throne
> Of the Invisible.... (Canto 4.1639-45)

As seen in both passages, Romantics often describe stunning experiences of nature's beauty as the "sublime" – a moment, experience, or encounter that touches who they are, their emotions and psyches, too deeply to be adequately expressed in words.

Though these particular lines by Romantic poets closely parallel my own philosophy on nature, these passages are not representative of the major Romantics' tendency toward pantheism. While their passion for nature's beauty sometimes moves Romantics to deify nature itself, my experiences and observations of nature inevitably lead me to wonder and worship of the Creator who must be behind it all. So as much as my poems are a tribute to one of nature's most stunningly beautiful places, they are equally a labor of love for the beauty of the Creator—and the Creator of beauty.

I come to Jocassee because the sublime is here. I come to Jocassee because Christ the sublime Creator is evident to me here, Christ whom Paul called "the image of the invisible God, the firstborn of all creation" (Col 1:15) and of whom Paul stated "For by him all things were created, in the heavens and on the earth, things visible and things invisible.... all things have been created through him, and for him. He is before all things, and in him all things are held together" (Col 1:16,17). The writer of Hebrews makes a similar claim in Chapter 1 (verses 2 and 3), and John presents Jesus in this manner: "In the beginning was the Word, and the Word was with God, and the Word was God. The same was in the beginning with God. All things were made through him. Without him was not anything made that has been made" (John 1:1-3). Thus, when I see beauty at Jocassee, I "see into the life of things," to borrow Wordsworth's phrase. And when I see into the life of things, I see the Spirit of Christ still at work renewing and sustaining the beauty of his creation. Therefore, my philosophy in this collection may aptly be described as Christian Romanticism.

In addition, my overarching themes best align with ideas held by some thinkers in Christian Mysticism. There were mystics such as St. Francis and Bonaventure who believed, as William Harmless puts it, that "If God is an artist, and creation is his artwork, then Christ is the Father's Artistry, the medium through whom all his artistic output is poured out . . . so that all creation reflects, whether clearly or dimly, the stamp of Christ" (*Mystics* 103). Harmless explains Bonaventure's particular view on the function of creation in facilitating our knowledge of God:

> [I]n his *Collations on the Six Days*, [Bonaventure] remarks that before Adam's Fall, creation was an open book: its lettering was clear, easily decipherable, so that 'through its representations, humankind was carried up to God.' To see God, the first couple simply read the book of creation. But with Adam's Fall, 'that book, namely the world, now seemed as if it were a dead letter, deleted, scribbled over.' With Christ's coming and with a new book, the scriptures, the book of creation became legible again. For Bonaventure, spiritual progress thus begins with reading God's presence through the book of creation, rediscovering its lucid calligraphy. (93)

Paul refers to such rediscovery in Romans, declaring "the invisible things of him since the creation of the world are clearly seen, being perceived through the things that are made, even his everlasting power and divinity . . ." (1:20). Perhaps this Pauline passage and Bonaventure's ideas inspired Coleridge, the most orthodox major Romantic, who in "Frost at Midnight" outlines his hope that his son will grow up with nature as a guide to perceiving God:

> But *thou*, my babe! shalt wander like a breeze
> By lakes and sandy shores, beneath the crags
> Of ancient mountain, and beneath the clouds,
> Which image in their bulk both lakes and shores
> And mountain crags: so shalt thou see and hear
> The lovely shapes and sounds intelligible
> Of that eternal language, which thy God
> Utters, who from eternity doth teach
> Himself in all, and all things in himself.
> Great universal Teacher! he shall mould
> Thy spirit, and by giving make it ask. (54-64)

In such a spirit, I have written this poetic collection at this time because in our culture, the need to notice nature has become much more desperate. I'd call it dire: the need of a desire and then ability to see clearly the "eternal language" of God behind the sublime creation that still, despite all the pollution by and disregard from humankind, shines forth His eternal glory continually renewed. If Coleridge saw this need with his culture in the throes of the Industrial Revolution, then most twenty-first century citizens face an exponentially greater struggle for this vision, needing the call to wander outside to read God's book of nature infinitely more – now.

∼

2. Revelation of a Double Mind

What does it mean – to love a place? There could be a number of answers. We might love a place where we feel at home, at ease;

have a sense of refuge; find a place that renews or restores us, or even a place that challenges us and makes us better in some way. To love deeply a place means we would feel devastated if the place was radically altered, transformed to be unrecognizable, or even totally erased. My love of Jocassee and its surrounding old-growth forest involves all of these. I have a sense of ownership that makes me feel at home the moment I arrive. As evidenced in the poems, I want to know the place down to its smallest element and mineral composition and widen out to the highest, broadest perspective of the lake and its rivers in order to try to see its expanse all at once. The poems record my attempts to do both, and every approach in between. My method of sharing the beauty of the place includes sharing specifics: names of rivers, creeks, mountains, islands, and spots on the lake; typical characteristics such as seasonal events, weather, and wind patterns; specific plants and trees; and specific animals and birds found here. Out of passion for the place, I have wanted to capture every detail.

However, in the course of researching how the lake was created, I had to realize that I was not the first to love this place with such devotion. Far from it. I also had to realize that for those who loved the place before I did, long before the valley was flooded to form the lake, the possibility of being devastated that one's place could be radically and forever changed, that one's place could disappear, had actually come to be – for many, and on multiple occasions. The Lower Cherokee clans who lived in the valley were ultimately driven out of this, their actual home, in the 1700s. Then much later, families who lived here were forced out when Duke Power gained rights to build the hydroelectric project that created the lake in the late 1960s, early 1970s. How difficult – perhaps impossible – to reconcile this knowledge of the painful loss for those who loved this place before, with my current zeal for what this valley has become in lake form!

When I was nearly finished with the poems, I had an experience that I believe was meant to cause me to think much more deeply about what it means to claim Jocassee as mine. Citizens of the Cherokee Nation have traditionally viewed birds as messengers from the Creator. I am highly inclined to agree that one or more birds may serve this function when we need comfort, reassurance of God's presence, or greater awareness of truths, complexities, or shortsightedness.

I think I had such a visit just after writing the next-to-last poem of this book. To relate the story, I will give a bit of background. I have always liked owls, but in recent years, screech owls or small owls in particular have taken on a very special meaning for me. This collection of poems was written during a time of great loss, grief, and personal transition. After a period of decline and illness of 12 years (during which he refused all medical care or medication in spite of significant pain), my father died in June 2016. In order to help care for Daddy near the end of his life, my husband and I sold our home, resigned a church where he was pastor, and left a community and neighbors we loved. I also resigned my career after 17 years of teaching college students, deciding to make a change even though I had spent over a decade earning 3 college degrees in that field and was unsure what to do next. So, this book took shape in the process of working through the grief of my father's long, traumatic illness and his passing, as well as trying to make sense of all other major changes and losses of the same year.

Strange as it might seem, two owls had given me comfort during that time: one – a necklace with a hand-carved screech owl pendant that I purchased on a day trip to Cherokee, NC, while Daddy was still sick, and two – a stuffed owl puppet (a burrowing owl, about the same size as a screech owl) that I purchased the day after my father died. Walking about the store that day in the stunned, numb state of shock and grief when intermittent waves of pain and sorrow rolled over us at unpredictable intervals, my husband and I had stumbled upon that puppet. It was ridiculously cute, and made us laugh until we cried. I had to buy it. Sometimes during the nights of grieving, I held the puppet as I slept.

The next year, I was able to take a one-day course on Introduction to Wildlife Rehab taught by Carlton Burke through the naturalist curriculum offered by The NC Arboretum of Asheville. And what was the animal we happened to witness first as we toured the May Wildlife Rehab Center at Lees-McRae College? A screech owl, of course, an ailing one that had just been brought in. We were able to watch his entrance exam as workers tried to determine the source of his hurt. He looked so small, diminished, with his feathers drawn in taunt with pain. I was deeply moved and prayed for the little being to recover. After I came home, I spent a few nights on our porch listening to screech owls calling in nearby trees. I mimicked their calls, trying to draw one closer.

So, with such interest in owls, a week after the visit to the wildlife rehab center, I wrote the second-to-last poem of this book and featured a screech owl in a prominent instance, the climactic point of the poem's events, in which an owl looks a man eye to eye at a moment of insight and healing. Then – one week to the day after I wrote that poem, an actual screech owl showed up over my car in our garage in broad daylight – looking *me* eye to eye! Though it is extremely rare to see one of these creatures in the daytime, he stayed for two days. Then he was gone. The timing of the visit gave me pause. I came to consider it a sign that 1) I needed to think more deeply about the complexities of so fervently loving this lake created at such great pain to others, and 2) I needed to revise several works to reflect the complexities more directly. Thinking on the visit, I also wrote the following poem called *Prelude:* Double Mind to outline the effect the owl in my garage had on my mindset. For this poem, as well as many others throughout the collection, I have provided a Notes section at the back of the book to help readers understand things such as place names, historical events, and terms such as "trail tree" not defined in the dictionary. So, use the notes in the back to help clarify terms in this poem inspired by the owl visit:

Prelude: Double Mind

I wrote a poem toward the end,
about things angels desire to look into,
about a screech owl messenger
of healing to hurting man –
Then, seven days to the day,
a screech owl, one of the lords of night,
actually appeared
over my car in the garage
mid-sunshine.
Wondrous
weird
stunning sight!

We stared long at one another.
I chattered to him awkwardly
telling him of his beauty
telling him I was glad he came.
He mesmerized me silently,
though clearly he had somewhat to say.
His eyes could have been
the deep deep pools that now cover Ellijay
where Whitewater River still converges with Toxaway
or those where Thompson and Whitewater
meet to undulate.

I first took him as a sign,
perfect timing,
confirmation on that poem
I'd just made,
affirmation of what I'd created
in these pages.
Two days, that owl stayed
in my shed then disappeared back

into the dark opaque.
But his eyes remained.
For weeks I prayed,
still lost in that rich, mysterious gaze,
trying to make sense
of what this nocturnal bird meant
coming in brightness of day
showing red phase.
I wanted to take him as good omen.
Yet when I began to revise,
to see my own work with new eyes,
I saw more fully what it means,
what it implies, to claim Jocassee as mine.

So now I see my double mind –
(Am I unstable
in all my ways, then?)
Fast as wind changes,
Jocassee became my spiritual haven.
But I see clearly now
that if traditions, artifacts, even native grave
mounds had not been desecrated,
this lake I love
would never have been created.

Yet one woman
I would have been
and I remain powerless
now to change it.
I revere this place.
Should I celebrate it?

This locale has always been sacred:
Long before valley flooded by lake,
Sacred to The Cherokee who lived
at Jocassee Town and Ellijay

and dipped in cleansing Whitewater River
seven times to begin each day,
Sacred to those baptized there
after they found The Way,
and though radically altered
by these fathoms of water,
Sacred now to ones like me.

Oh, for a trail tree
to point this modest poet
towards how to write these lines
prayerfully
respectfully
to render the beauty of pure waters
fallen on my sight like copious rain
ever trickling, crashing
Blue Wall cliffs above Jocassee,
to write my love of this location
and creatures here
but to trivialize no one's pain.
Can this be achieved?

Three centuries past,
The Lower Cherokee clans
lived at confluence
of Whitewater and Toxaway
Rivers in this valley.
Now, here I am,
confluence of red skin
and white skin,
ultimately a product
of what's been done.

I see the lake's core
on fire at dusk with setting sun.

> Does the fire come both from above
> and from deep down?
> For I see rising 6000 bushels of flaming corn
> stored years by diligent native hands
> torched now at Ellijay council house
> by shallow greedy men.
> Frenzy for land –
> Oh, sagacious owl,
> Is that where I began?

After the screech owl visit, my poems still celebrate the beauty of the lake as it is, but I am most definitely conflicted. While Jocassee has become a sanctuary for me in every sense of the word, I am deeply sorry for those who (as I state in the collection's opening poem, Jocassee's Mine) are "forever, insatiably homesick for a place that no longer exists". Now, while I do come here to worship, play, wonder, and be recharged, I am always mindful of the pain, wrong, and loss as well. So, on these matters, I remain inevitably double-minded.

From the early poem titled Mediator to the closing poem, these poems move in a loose overall progression from grief and loss to revelation, salvation, communion with God through nature's beauty, battles of faith versus fear, to final ultimate rest. I hope the poems inspire outdoor adventures. I hope they encourage time on the water. I hope they motivate thought and further research about Jocassee and the surrounding areas of Pickens and Oconee Counties in South Carolina, and Transylvania and Jackson Counties in North Carolina. I hope they fuel curiosity about this sublime natural world in general, for the boundaries of these poems sometimes do broaden well beyond Jocassee to include water and creatures worldwide. I hope they provoke wonder about science, about the marvel of every living creature, about beauty, about how to find hope and serenity. Above all, I hope they inspire a thirst to know the One who made and sustains it all, keeping water in constant motion ~ everywhere.

3. Reading Poetry: A Few Tips for
Enjoyment and Understanding

~

A. Whenever possible, read poetry aloud. If there is no punctuation (no period, no comma, no semicolon, no colon) at the end of a line of poetry, then there is no pause. So, if there is no punctuation at the end of a line, then you should keep right on reading into the beginning of the next line without slowing or pausing.

B. Read a poem more than once. First, read for an overall sense of the situation as to what is happening in the poem, without slowing down if you come to an unfamiliar word or reference. On the second reading, note any words, phrases, references, names, or place names unfamiliar to you. Looking up their meanings in a dictionary or finding further information can be a major help to your enjoyment of the poem and its themes. **Remember, the back of this book also includes a Notes section (organized by poem titles) providing definitions and explanations of some non-dictionary terms such as objects, names of people, historical events, and places to aid your understanding and to inspire your own research and further reading.** Reread poems a third time (or more) with your new knowledge for an enhanced understanding of their messages.

C. One of my favorite aspects of poetry is that it often highlights word play – the ways that words have rich meanings, the way the same word can resonate with multiple meanings that sometimes bring humor or enriched insight to a passage because of layered shades of definition, referring to several ideas, objects, events, or people all in one word or expression, all at once. For example, in my poem titled Destiny on page 27, the phrase "in light drops" in the first line has multiple possibilities of meaning: since it comes after "water falls," then "drops" can refer to the motion of the water going downward, or to the individual particles or droplets of water themselves; the word "light" that comes before "drops" can refer to the rays of the sun by which we see water falling, or to the quality of how a droplet of water does not weigh much when considered individually. In addition, the phrase "in light" calls to mind the phrase "in light of," which we use to make meaning of our experiences, and it relates thematically to the poem, which explores how we often are not able to see how individual experiences are meant to be, when viewed "in light of" our overall destiny. Considering such possibilities of multiple word meanings typically enhances your experience of reading poems. Language's ambiguity helps make poetry challenging, entertaining, and profound.

~

II

Jocassee's Mine

Though I've not yet notified
proper authorities –
neither The Cherokee Nation,
nor descendents of Jocassee Valley generations,
neither Duke Power, DNR,
the esteemed Governor of South Carolina,
nor National Geographic –
Though I've not told any of these,
Lake Jocassee is officially – mine.

I intend no imperialist's claim.
For me, it's a spiritual thing.
Please - Let me explain.

No bill of sale or legal deed,
I've paid no money down,
signed no mortgage.
I've no document of inheritance,
no tangible family right
no centuries-old stake in the place,
though the blood of both Cherokee
and European settler streams my veins.
I have not given my life
for this property,
not even incrementally,
as one works hour on hour,
day on day, year on year,
decade on decade
to finally say – it's mine.

Nor have I paid
the price of a heart
forever, insatiably
homesick for a place
that no longer exists.

This place has been loved then taken before.
I've not been charged the bitter tears
of these who must have felt in their core
the loss of Jocassee Town, Ellijay –
and much later Attakulla Lodge's valley
now flooded beneath these depths.
This lake irretrievably erased
Whitewater River Valley's falls and shoals
except in evanescent memories of those
who knew every bend, every rock, every pool.
The place has always been consecrated:
To The Cherokee who bathed
facing east in this pure vibrant river
seven times to begin in strength each day –
To those who later communed there
with living water at baptizing hole,
To those who thirst to drink to their toes
an ice cold, soul-soothing taste
from Whitmire spring if only just once more.
This water – this river current of power that still flows
though now submerged beneath this lake's deep
is revered anew by ones like me.
I honor all these who lost their place,
who still ache to re-member
beauty that used to be.

Likewise, just as I've not earned Jocassee
at cost of such painful loss,
I cannot claim supreme ownership
inherent to being creator of a thing.
I did not engineer or build the dams
that form and preserve this lake,
and certainly did not shape
her raw watery elements.
I hold no patent on what mystifying teal
permeates her pure mineral deep
(far above Duke Energy stands that Higher Power

who formed much more than 1.5 billion cubic kilometers
of liquid molecules
and brought light upon the face of fathoms.
Jocassee has always existed
in the mind of the One
who devised and divides primordial waters).

My ownership proves
hard to see or touch:
passion in my voice
when I'm packing my boat to go,
or my countenance
newly wed to serenity when I return ~ amazed ~
illuminated by spiritual rays
buoyant from expeditions to her holy sights
blessed by encounters with her creature life.
These proofs are immaterial, unquantified,
yet no less real
than a legal document that binds.

It's the sort of love
that made Swift and Yeats
long for Ireland though called to work in London
and Thomas praise his childhood Wales
no matter who thought it wild, untamed, isolated.
It's Burns's Highlands,
Wordsworth's Grasmere,
Shelley's Mont Blanc,
The Brontës' Moor,
Thoreau's Pond,
Dillard's Tinker Creek,
Arnow's Kentucky,
Wolfe's Asheville.
The places continually carried in their souls
were their spiritual homes,
owned by and defining the essence
of who they were.

This is Jocassee for me –
Jocassee's mine!
Oh – but the glory
of psychological ownership:
This liquid, emerald crown
of South Carolina,
can belong to you,
and you too.

A person who owns a piece of land
does not exclusively own the sky above it
any more than one legally owns
rays of sun
that grow one's trees,
rain in the act
of falling upon one's grass,
or the color green.
Some riches like water belong to us all,
by existential laws of living.
Paradox, then, when I claim Jocassee
and say you may do the same?
No, if you ache for the place,
you'll know what I mean.
Lake Jocassee is mine
as the Blue Ridge Mountains
and the Southern Appalachians
are mine.
She is mine, like my day off,
my private thoughts,
my community,
and the fresh rural air I breathe.

So, come with me –
Let's paddle rhythmically
on this shimmering dark aquamarine –
I hope you'll see.

See –
how the Spirit of God still moves
upon the face of the waters.

Come –
Explore where four wild, splashing rivers
Whitewater, Thompson, Toxaway, Horsepasture
and creeks, their baby sisters,
begin high as mountain trickles
then grow to tumble steep gorges
down Blue Ridge Escarpment
North Carolina south
to whisper slow peace to Keowee River
still rolling under lake's deep.

Delight –
in creatures who hunt here and thrive here.
Beautiful drama to watch them
survive, to watch them play,
They own it too, and just as fully.

I want to see the life here,
to count Jocassee's beings
from tiniest blue damselflies
to great herons and bald eagles,
wild boars, black bears
and white-tailed deer.
I want to bless them where they live.
They are pure in heart;
They see God.

Come, my friends,
though there's haunting beauty here.
Aren't most places humans think they own
shadowed by irreparable wrongs?

Come with me,
for I want to paddle across Devil's Fork,
riding glinting ripples of submerged memories
(and wicked, emotional undercurrents
intrinsic to living)
to where Whitewater River
now falls into this lake.

I want to bask on a Jocassee island,
all to ourselves,
slip off Jackie's Branch icy rock waterslide shelf
or leap off cliff ledge at Laurel Fork Falls
into water
so quickening
we'll feel born again. Again.

With curiosity and zeal of the explorer,
and unsurpassed love
and intimate knowledge of the native,
I want to be fully immersed
in this numinous place,
and to share it with you –
cautiously, though – mindful that
explorers turn to pillagers,
and natives can take for granted.

But Jocassee ardor
awakens the conscience
of an owner
who *owns* her –
not on paper but in depths of a person,
bound to protect her like a first-born child.
I own Jocassee this way.
You can too.

Mediator

Even a liquid surface can tire the feet:
footfall on footfall, as water falls, as
tinkling droplets returning to their source
slide from the soles. So I took to my boat.
Some wrongly thought I had found him long ago,
the love torn apart by my father's house.
How could they bury a young woman's grief
beneath 340 feet of water?
The river at least had been crossable.
But I began sinking, seeking him
while the waters started to rise,
my tears falling undiscerned into this
new lake born of five rivers.
My boat mediates now - between the water and me.

The Venture

What is she doing out here alone
on water so deep, so remote?
Strange fishermen could take her body,
unconcerned for her heart.
Yet we see her in morning mist
steadily crossing broadest stretch of lake.
Has she been here all night?
A woman venturing out by her self,
a woman who most fears living in fear,
can be quite disquieting.
But with pure soul
made worthy by faith
made strong by suffering,
she takes her quest
and paddles to survive.

Austere Miles
a villanelle

I saw your pain but couldn't change a thing
then rowed for harsh and austere miles today.
I found no solace from the suffering.

Catfish pulled from the deep, left dead to gleam,
crow robbed the nest before young birds could play.
I saw your pain but couldn't change a thing.

I could have helped the locust on his wings
wriggling, desperate to leave the lake and fly.
I had no solace for the suffering.

The bass will eat the locust in the stream.
Mad hornets from the hive will swarm one day.
I saw your pain but couldn't change a thing.

The trials of Job, and Joseph sold for rings,
I closed the book; what matters if I pray?
I found no solace from the suffering.

I think of you, my father, and I sing
and row for harsh and austere miles this way.
I saw your pain but couldn't change a thing.
Was there a reason for your suffering?

Destiny

Water falls – in light drops
at first as slow as snow flurries,
swallowed by bodies of lakes
and oceans nestling two-thirds of earth's face.
Water – always moving, changing form and pace,
seeking to get to the bottom of things.
Who knew? Who could imagine
the Atlantic waves from which you raised me
in your arms when I was seven
would comprise the very same water that now,
having made its destined passage through the great cycle,
decades since, slips quietly from my kayak paddles
as they part the surface of this bluer lake?

Tacking

I'm making a sudden turn –
from where I was headed
back to the beginning,
to a place I can't even imagine.
I've rowed strenuously
for hours under indifferent sun,
squinting to find this very stream.
I tore muscle fibers paddling here.
Consistently, it hurt.
My boat has neither sail nor motor;
My propeller has been sheer torque of will.
Why would I turn around now,
and not row upstream
as far as my flatwater boat can go?

If I continue in this direction,
there could be waterfalls,
reddest Indian paintbrush,
bear drinking at riverbank,
best thing ever seen,
just around the bend.
This explorer has never
failed to hate the turn-around,
abandon-course,
the circle-back.
Could I not go one mile more
and stop to hear a woodpecker
work her frantically decreed circle
on hollow hemlock, next hill?

But no, it's the loons I hear now,
telling one another
how darkness is coming.
Their call sounds mournful to me,
probably not to them.
Perhaps it's a comfort to them:
a ritual performed religiously
at regular intervals,
to keep things moving along
doing what loons do
to live and thrive as loons.
This evening, it's a signal I must heed,
for my boat has no light,
and Jocassee dark
is wilderness dark –
and when time is right, outer space dark.

Long before human thought,
before Earth's water ripe for life,
even Jupiter and Saturn (by omniscient Might)
reversed orbital motions at crucial point –
great sailboats tacking into the wind,

ordering our solar system
conditions – then life could begin.

So, I change direction
and start again.
The place where I began
will be different to me now
because I am now different.
Of course, earnest exertion
has inherent purpose.
While we make our journeys,
our journeys make us.
In healing overtaxed fibers,
muscles grow strongest,
and the human will,
chiefest muscle of who we are,
accomplishes no great thing
until challenged, broken,
and challenged again.
There's just no getting anywhere
without coming from somewhere,
and if my somewhere
ripped muscles and taxed eyes
and stressed will
and drained sweat
down face and back,
(our galaxy has a violent past)
at least it left me thirsty –
perfect –
because regarding the tack:
Wherever I'm going,
I'm certain
there's plenty of water.

slow fin parts surface
Jocassee carp emerges
like pain from the deep

Deep

Don't we all sometimes feel
so uncalled for?
But deep always calls to deep,
like depth of this lake
to depth of my soul.
A soul, after all, must be similar
to these inscrutable fathoms:
Divers, you'll freeze blue
without a suit
to cover you,
and a tank
full of the breath of life,
and it's black down there –
Deep and dark are
often very close sisters –
bring the light!
Warmth and breath
and light must be
brought there
if we hope to survive.

I am a body of water
on this body of water,
my body over half comprised
of this transparent liquid.
I am buoyant.
Am I see-through?
As newborns,
we're over three-fourths water,

but down to 65% by age one
(trailing clouds of glory
do we come)
souls
apart from the Creator,
drier and less watery
they become.
So we live and grow
increasingly thirsty
for a place
to swim and once again
be in over our heads.

I always have water
on my mind:
my human brain
73 % water.
The living water –
all around me
is in me too.
Deep calls to deep,
the call to drink,
an inaudible sound,
spiritual waves
heard on the frequency
of mind and soul,
ethereal acoustics.
He who has ears
to hear
let him hear
the call of deep water
to deep.

a piece of pure lake
has broken loose to frolic
as Eastern bluebird

Broken

Again I wonder
paddling Lake Jocassee:
Where are those little songsters
who take forest limb stages
and trill joy of being
from eager beaks?
Sure, almost every visit
I see birds who shriek:
ratchety complaints,
great herons stomp sky;
kingfishers scold irritated screech
as I wreck fishing night.
Sometimes, I even see bald eagles
rise on plaintive whys
to pose in shortleaf pines.
But songbirds?

Today, the answer comes
in stillness.
Shady cove, I tie my boat
to beached log and sit inside,
body, vessel bobbing rise
and fall, waves sometimes gentle,
sometimes rapid
wake of motorcraft.
In quiet, thinking I have gone,
out come titmouse
and frenetic gray squirrel,
out come cardinal and thrush –

into maple sanctuary, thickest laurel bush
on water's shore,
chirruping and warbling and getting happy
as if they'd just sung down the end of all war.

But when squirrel runs down tree
and locks eyes with mine,
his chatter announces my presence
with echo that seems to warn
every creature that will ever be.
Just as quickly, they all disappear.
All goes quiet again
except distant boats, buzz of speed.
With the sigh of Eve leaving the garden,
I wonder in that grove
where my very presence has stopped the music:
When will we lose this curse of fear
and be able to live like friends again?

Not Drifting

"And what are you doing here
double-crested cormorant,
nomad on this mountain lake
water of plankton sheen
floating a not-yet-spiral galaxy?"

"Not drifting. Waiting…." he said,
phyto-green eyes anticipating
elements expelled from stars that burn
sure return of northwest breeze
rushing back to coast and sea.

Water on the Line

1
Water everywhere on the line,
borders, porous, flow:

Between Georgia and South Carolina:
Chattooga to Yoneh from Tugaloo
meets Jocassee to Keowee to Hartwell
to fuse with Savannah River, fluid
state boundary always moving

And it's a liquid divide,
US Mexican Rio Grande
(where they'll insist on fracking
even in water-stressed time).

In New York, Niagara River defines
Canadian US margin sublime –
though we share the falls, equal wonder to all.

Both Brazil and Argentina claim
mighty River Iguazu that cuts its name
between two countries into 275
cascades of white penetrable twine.

2
Trying to live pure in this contemporary world –
It's complicated.
Most of us complicit
Most of us contribute
to toxins in the water table.
Is it a watery gulf that segregates hell?
Will all water we ever polluted
forever form that underworld's well?

But surely there's someone like me,
parched to taste human unity, simple decency?
Turn off the news. It's toxic.
Please, will someone purify the drinking water with
      moringa seeds?
Fact is, we're all tributaries.

3

Why can't it be this easy?
I put my two fingers, right hand,
on Google Maps
and expand.
– State lines irritate my mind –
I wish them gone,
and mystically ~
border lines,
state names melt,
city names disappear ~
The only lines left
watery
rivers
(Now the view is clear)
They've always been here ~
Before states
counties
governments
countries
Before us
Before maps,
the water cut
her lines
across the land
on her way from one sea to another,
her blue the veins
of continental bodies
her substance the blood
bringing life to and from the heart.

May Bees
on bees and ontology

Contemplate the whatness of a bee:
May, mining bees
lake bank,
quiet but not yet silent spring.
Handled too roughly,
they sting –
tiny in a massive scheme
of things.
Yet vitally important
to the web of beings.
Could our modifications
ruin blooms
they need?
Could we
doom ourselves
brushing off
honeyed wings?
Will we just miss
the sweetness?
Will we see
what this means?
May bee?
May be….

Cold Comfort
sestina for Debbie Fletcher

We moderns rarely understand the cold
of our ancestors, when winter, lusty for death,
forced them to build a fire or freeze by degrees.
Drinking the snow and avoiding the river,
September to March, slow nights, longing for spring.
Removing one's cloak to bathe? No doubt, a shock.

Radical change does mean traumatic shock,
like your first swim here, when you cried, "It's not cold!"
This lake lukewarm, not your whitewater spring,
to you was a graveyard, memento of death,
vanished valley and lost girlhood river
where swimming brought thrills at fifty degrees.

Progress improves life only to degrees.
hydroelectric dams – always a shock,
when we make a lake, we take a river
to warm our homes and banish the cold.
Current convenience often means the death
of a thing like a freshwater spring.

Once, kayaking this lake at early spring,
up Horsepasture River I moved in degrees
toward my source, mountain folk now touched by death.
As I rowed north, my bare feet sensed a shock:
through my boat, I felt water grow frost cold
at the point where lake forms from pure river.

What happens when we swim in frigid rivers?
We gasp! Then electrical currents spring
from our nerves to our brains with jolt of cold.
Blood pumps deeper. We fire up fine degrees.
Small-scale hydroelectric power shock:
for now, we cheat Jordan's chilly water of death.

Shivering not with cold but dread of memories' death,
you cried for us all when you wept for your river.
Facing erasure of what matters most brings shock,
that for our past cold indifference might spring,
that traces of our places would melt by degrees.
It's heat that travels – what can't move is cold.

But hope in slow-moving cold wet atoms thwarts death.
Diving gave you chills, deep degrees: Near your steadfast river?
The past lodged! From lake floor springs a peaceful shock!

Warm Marrow

Mountains themselves
form a Wide M
going up, going down,
going up, going down –
a series of
Majestics
Mine

Turned upside-down?
They Make a W,
wounded with scars
of Machines going down to dig
and up to haul out their hearts—
Wasteland
Mined....

....Then filled with Water like giant cups
       from Which We creatures drink sunshine

Palindrome Dreams

How many palindromes are in this poem?
Not nearly as many as the joys one sees
when one solos in a kayak dewed
with sweat any sweet Lake Jocassee noon.
One does not have to consult dad or mom
or the shahs of the senate
to discover this basic tenet.
One does not have to pull up in a 1991 Civic
to hear sagas that could repaper
a world of touch screens.
One does not have to peep from a race car
with one's face getting progressively redder
to know what a wreck is
in the drama of the sexes.
One does not have to be Madam Sosostris
or be deified, put up a neon sign,
look through a third eye,
or listen to Abba with Anna
while drinking wine.
One does not have to buy a boat
with a rotor or even a rotator seat
or a fish-finding radar
when one is at water level
with a paddle on both ends
in one's hands.
One does not have to have
the expectations of Pip.
Did you catch all that?
Yes, ma'am, tit for tat.
Never odd or even,
I would refer to the stats on the success rate
for Hannah when she prayed –
a mighty deed indeed
from the great reviver
of seeds and dreams.

Catch and Release

I've just never been a fisherman.
I understand if you wish to call me weak,
but I've too much sympathy for the fish,
the live minnow bait, even the grasshoppers,
and I've rejoiced to see unused nightcrawlers
crawl back away into night freed.

But I once caught an ideal
no less beautiful than those two shockingly fast
lake trout that sped by me (as I was about to swim
at Turtleback Island cross from Double Springs),
their bodies long and lean and sleek
as wingless jets.

I spent arduous hours
drawing in that catch, aching neck and back,
mind reeling expense of pain.
A few times I let out singing line,
just let it run, unsure
I'd ever pull it close to bank again

Yet finally teasing it in, I held a prize in eager hands,
grateful, elated, captivated by spotted rosy rainbow.
Decades-long moment, so accomplished.
Then, tenacious flesh writhed to be free, struggled to breathe.
Seeing at last a realized dream is hard to keep, I lowered the
      marvel,
watching it swim to its heaven – released.

Ease

Will you call me guitarist
if I now make music in my dreams?
If right before I wake from sleep
my fingers chord the strings
with ease for friends and me?
Will you call me sailor
if I open my umbrella
and a wind's favor pulls
my kayak cross Jocassee's
choppy water from Laurel Fork
to Mill Creek?
Or Devil's Fork
to Double Springs?
If I know enough to know
I'll battle southwest headwind
to return from there after three?
Will you call me poet
if inspiration only
sporadically touches me
with insistent breeze?
If words rarely come together
quickly as I please?

The Point

I sigh and squint and stare at the point
across Jocassee's widest water
flecked with shimmers.
I fear I'll never get there
as an unblinking sun
tans me, ears to thighs,
with his radiant eye.
I pause to drift and stay
small waterfalls that salt my face.

Starting again, I find my pace,
right, left, right – glide,
right, left, right – glide,
I see the steady stir of white liquid
motion at my kayak's sides:
The lake is proud of her loveliness –
She wants me to notice
how Coriolis plays in little circles
when my paddles break her surface.

I look up to see the point now;
I've been lifted there somehow
by this beautifully tsunamic
yet gently swelling
wave of mindfulness –
a point in time.
It's an old truth, perpetually learned
by souls like mine:
By the way, beauty is the point.

Hardy

2016
April's surprise
winter-enduring vine
wild honeysuckle
encircling
climbs
laurel limbs
up rock cliffs
winding
like time
adorning
this lake's solitary beach:
beautiful sight to me.
Surviving eradication
from subdivisions,
nuisance weed's
black seeds
carried here
by dauntless birds,
tough yellow
blossoms stretch
from shades
of steep mountain
to reach
Carolina sun.

1926
Unwanted girl
placed in public square
Eastern Kentucky
age three
stained yellow dress
pitch
black hair
Take her if you please.
Strong constitution
growing up
hard
working
tobacco fields
binding burley leaves
with twine
finding love
then alcohol
when he died
young
leaving her and their nine
children behind.
Hardy spirit,
how often did she dream
of morning glories
tightly wound
around tobacco stalks?
The men had cursed
their stubborn coils;
She just loved
their blooms.

eight-inch turtle head
surfaces then slowly sinks –
just an illusion?

Toward Restitution

Mid-October
bare feet in water
serene
under fire maple leaves
I whittle
a piece of driftwood
from the beach.

This boulder
where I sit:
remnant
of the blasts
that formed The Wall
and filled the dam.
This wood:
shard of pristine forest
sacrificed for this lake.
How long –
to make
a tree?
How long –
to erase
the woods?

I hear
the oaks
dropping acorns
behind me:
What noise
as they skitter down,
cross branches
off steep banks,
bounce off stones
and touch ground –
active as human seed
when it seeks to make life.
Imperceptible sound
compared to frenzied sawing
timber falling
and pleeeading horses
forced to pull out logs
for railcars bound toward town.
Some whole sections
not clear-cut in time
left standing,
covered upright
by waters that rose
to form lake's impound.

I turn back to the bank,
observe acorns,
play with them,
arrange them
in patterns
on the sand.
They glisten like amber
in this humid afternoon,
and I must
hold their bodies
of burnt umber

beige and dark green striations
with little mottled cup caps
in my hand,
as when a child.

But suddenly –
I don't know why –
I toss, offhand,
the largest one
into a dark, hard crevice
in the boulders.

That acorn,
My albatross.

Risking snakebite,
I reach in and stretch
to grasp it again.
Holding up to light
between my fingers,
I kiss its skin
and place back
in leafy dirt
up on the bank
where it
might
just
send down
anchoring roots –
then, stretch up
auspicious young shoots.

Reach

*"We do not have knowledge of a thing until we
have grasped its why, that is to say, its cause"* ~ Aristotle

Rumble
radiates outward from a storm
over Toxaway River,
place of thunder,
and I am
struck
by an idea:

Rivers
flow in one direction -
yet at Bad Creek
they make
the river flow backwards
up tunnel
through mountain.

Rest.
There's more.
An object at rest will stay at rest.
An object in motion will stay in motion
along a straight line
unless acted upon
by an unbalanced outside force.

Reverent,
leaning on this massive slab
of old Toxaway gneiss,
the seasoned hunter says
he's never, not once, seen an arrow
shoot itself through the air.
I believe him.

Receded
into the distance, mountains further,
then further away
look progressively hazier, fainter blue gray.
Closer hills, more distinctly we perceive.
But how often do we focus on the light itself
which allows us to see?

Roots
of desperate trees
hang starving, gnarly,
soil eroded
yanked by gravity
along lake banks
ripped from beneath.

Rainwater
caught in grandmother's barrel
to water her flowers.
Hurry! Hurry!
Sprinkle the marigolds.
There's a hole in our bucket.
We leak.

Reeling,
a wild turkey furiously pecks
his own reflection
on my truck's front bumper
for half a day
then presently walks away, face unchanged.
Hard, hard as steel – these laws of physics:

Ride
on
the one-directional
arrow of time.
You'll find
entropy increases,
free energy decreases.

Rush!
Speed equals distance divided by time.

Race:
When an object is acted upon
by unbalanced outside force,
it will accelerate.

Rapid!
1916, and how soon
did they hear the rumble of Toxaway River
thirty-foot squall of water
speeding seven miles down gorge
pulling death's prickly black blanket,
trees and silt smothering Cane Brake valley?

Remember,
of the eyes
that witnessed
that flood
and survived,
not one still sees -
at least not on this side.

Reaction.
For every action,
there is an equal
but opposite
reaction.

Rowing
upstream is entirely possible.
You might paddle to the lake's farthest reach,
even to the footbridge over Toxaway,
but it will take quite a span of time.
By your arm strength alone,
you won't get there at speed of light.

Raised
from the earth, native arrowheads
you pick up while stretching your legs at Cane Brake,
side by side on your kayak: white quartz, flint black
barbs, serrated edges,
tips still sharp enough -
deadly work - beautiful purpose.

Resurrected,
the widow's son kisses Elisha's cheek
and rushes out
to sell more
of that oil
that never runs dry -
like this creek.

Finding Fault
Spiritual Tectonics

If an earthquake caused a dam break,
who would be at fault?
The power company?
Watchdogs because they couldn't
make people believe?
Nature? God? You or me?
Fate or design?
Incremental ravages of time?

.....Thinking along these fault lines

Fault: complicated, vexed matter indeed.
All victims of one system
or another, predecessor,
abusive sister or brother,
we're all deeply cracked,
jagged, fractured to the core –
so much on our ancestral plate –
and victims beget victims

while hurt fans out concentric
circles as the instigating pebble
slips down, down
sinks slowly through resistant water
to the ground underneath
rarely seen again.
Then dozens of puzzled
offspring come paddling

unsuspecting into this ripple zone
where nature perpetuates
inherited faults, and for good measure,
adds a few unique ones of our own.
So for each generation
doesn't it get increasingly complicated
since we've collectively built such places
over perilously-positioned spaces?

    ….No one was ignorant of water's potential devastation

Are lines of culpability
blurred as they seem?
Assigning blame,
we'd look into what's left of the lake
to see reflections of our own
genetically-shaped faces.
In each of us there is a fissure
much deeper and older

than Brevard Fault Zone beneath these five
Southern states. Yesterday, again, earth quaked
in Augusta, deep underneath the Georgia line
and tremored here too, Devil's Fork Campground.
Little wonder – when faulty people come together
colliding on this metamorphic terrain,
the epicenter is everywhere.
Aren't we bound for earthquakes and dam breaks all around?

A Start
to a broadhead skink

When you sidled out on your rock
to bask in east Jocassee sun
right next to my elbow as I paddled by,
I started.

I jumped out of my skin
and into a spirit of wonder
to see a new thing under the sun –
a new thing to me.

I never knew you existed
never knew how that to keep your kind existing
your head swells grotesquely orange
to attract a mate – it's your way.

Most people don't want to see you.
You're repulsive and revolting to those
who would lock you deep in a den.
Give us a chickadee singing endearingly, we say –
                                that's our way.

So when I saw you, I started
out of my shell and into my spirit
to see things hiding under the rock in me:
unsightly things – sour, dour, unholy.

I see them slink into the light
knowing I should both fight and flee them,
but I can't take flight from the sight of them,
And that's a start.

now that the scales have
fallen, what will you show me
through your creation?

Living Water

"Come see a man I just met who told me
all things I ever did!" she said,
with gleaming countenance
almost unbearable to behold
but too exquisite, too graceful to dismiss –
so they came running to see indeed.

And here, this mother otter and three
exuberant young ones testify of him too:
"Come and see!" they say with every
playful undulation in this cool,
luminous, holy cove, "Come and taste
the living water. He is good!"

What's New?
sestina for the sages

Of course, there is a time for Solomon the sage
to convince us there's no new thing under the sun,
or for belated scholars to remind conquest-
minded Columbuses their New World wasn't really new,
or for paternal Prosperos, world-weary,
to caution precariously green Mirandas: 'tis only new to you.

Yet there's also a time to grant: if it's new to you,
it's new! We are rarely more perceptive, more sage,
than when we transport our bodies, workday weary,
to a water-blessed place under life-giving sun
where it's morning all day and perpetually new.
There, over the mundane, we make our conquest.

We're all starving for a visual conquest
when we thrill to see a sight like you,
little warbler, who today, to me, was new:
crown of yellow, midnight-spotted throat, wings of sage,
I gasped and stopped to watch you in mottled creek-bank sun.
Leaving with you new in mind, I'm no longer weary.

So, just beyond we've-seen-it-all brand of weary,
a fresh sight in nature makes its placid conquest.
A new creature rises before us like the sun,
and for the moment, Adam, we are you –
naming the first beings amid the first wood sage.
Those animals indeed were truly new.

And seeing You, God, will be – somehow – forever new.
Of seeing Your being – how could we weary?
Greatest of all newness? To see pure holiness, Almighty Sage!
It's a devoutly-to-be-wished conquest:
world of something always-about-to-be with You
when we'll no longer need the light of the sun.

But here, in light of all we ever knew of the sun,
our midbrains only fire when seeing something wholly new.
We seek this stimulation because we're drawn to You.
Toward any light stimulus leans the plant that's dark-weary.
Constant thirst for new proves we're made for eternal conquest
in transcendent, immortal fields of warblers over scarlet sage.

For now, between genesis and sage revelation, under waning sun,
our minds, wired for conquest, can be sustained by the new
in little birds, giving our weary souls sweet indications of You.

Welcome Home

Must I choose
between home here
or home beyond the blue?
There's a world for us to love,
a world that sometimes loves us too.
I've noticed. Have you?

I saw her linger in a cove
east of Corbin Creek.
More than once
she started to leave
then circled drifting back,
fingers skimming
May water playfully.
Why did she stroke this lake
so soothingly?

I follow the wake of beauty
somehow still visible to me
(her ghost - my final chance)
though a full day has passed.

Then I see

At least
twenty sparkling bluegill minnows,
iridescence in motion,
they look sideways at me
with innocent eyes
unschooled
in heron, hungry bass
or fishhook lures.
Swimming undulant, slow,
they wonder at this new
five-finned fish of my hand

gently plunged amongst them;
wildly naive, they almost taste my skin
with eager incessant infant mouths.

I begin to row out of the cove
but together they follow my kayak
as if singularly pulled by magnetic
maternal attraction –
Do they trail me because my boat is blue?
Because they want food?
Do they feel how I love them?
I still do.

No matter where I am,
I'm here forever too –
with bright aquatic eyes
fully looking
fully alive
telling me
Welcome home!
Welcome home!
We love you.
What took you so long?

Water Proof

You are waterproof,
naturally born buoyant.
Water doesn't saturate your body
and sink you right to the bottom.
Did you know it's possible
to be filled
with silence,
To hear silence
on a weekday
with Jocassee all to yourself,
To hear silence
permeate
and heal
you down to the cells?

So you are water proof –
How did you get that way,
formed of organic material,
mostly of clay?

Survival Course
Jocassee Rondeau

If by chance you find yourself left
in a stark pocket of lostness,
speck in forty thousand acres
around Jocassee's wild nature,
thirsty and starving beyond rest

beyond the grubs, tangled tress
cruel kudzu leaves, strange berries red,
seek the creek's cascading breakthrough.
There, being led, you'll find yourself

tracing creek to riverbed –
but shocked – you want to climb instead
of going down to speedboat saviors!
Trace river upward to the place where
wisest thrive, rainfall and green-earth-fed.
There, at last, you'll find yourself.

Hold Your Fire

"Hold your fire!" I want to yell,
but instead I freeze in place.
After all, a man who'd randomly
fire six rounds
into this placid Jocassee forest
must be trapped in a heart of darkness.

Kayaking back from distant Bear Creek,
I'd seen water dropping from my oars
make slow-motion bullet holes in the lake,
peaceful, evanescent holes, water displaced,
fluid dynamic ruptures from my piercing ache
to know You in the beauty of holiness.

And from miles away, I've heard Thompson River
rush to meet this larger body.
Eye couldn't be satisfied until I paddled to see.
Awestruck, I longed for more, but night came falling.
Impossible to this mortal, but tantalizing:
to behold all a river's mighty cascades and its source at one time.
But ultimately, that's why I come here:
I want to hold Your fire.

Blue Wall Psalms

1

What happened at this place?
Creation devastates,
alters scapes, earth shapes.
Sublime unnatural lake sits this slip,
this river of rock, Jocassee Thrust Fault.
Changed – the course of the waters forever.

One triangular rock, one by two inches
Henderson Gneiss rigid minerals
fill a hundred tiny shimmering crystals:
visible evidence of fiery birth
that worked its way through sifted earth
to be loved, inspected on flesh of a hand.

Composed in heat of earth's fluid mind,
bits of microline, fine-grained muscovite ~
is it unwittingly they shine?
Minuscule crystals show burning minerals quickly stabilized.
Then, relatively soon in time, Israelite and Cherokee altar fires
on separate continents glowed constant flame which never died.

2

Lift your eyes, oh saints, to Carolina hills
streaming sources of this lake we float.
In fact, go closer. Climb up Blue Wall boulders.
Rock-hop to heights where crashing water falls. You'll
find in our carnal hardness
we've not praised Him nearly enough ~
next to these, we've scarcely praised Him at all.

So, up there, down steep gorges, hard-gneiss rocks cry out:
(if not for stones, we'd hardly hear the sound of water fall).
Listen: the watery eyes of the hills are audible.
To see their gorges all at once, perch wings of a bird,
access eye of God, or at least use Google Earth.
But best hike these four riversides. You'll be audience
to great cloud witnesses. Try it ~ try to distinguish
between loud water rushing rocks, or vast elated human crowd
wildly clapping holy applause. It's hard.
Rocks and racing rivers together bless Him like saints canonical,
like ancient prophets with fire-furnaced bones they shout,
"If you won't praise Him, we will! We shall!"
with the feeling of rough high mountains,
"Hear our craggy Blue Wall Psalms!"

3

See me: Toxaway River, 21-mile long-suffering, patient saint,
I seemed a river damned, forced to flow between two dams,
but devoted, I've kept the way of praise though slain, scoured
to bedrock August 1916 by cruel flood, fault of rain and man.
Hear my sacred hymns: Stone banks etched in thin grooves sheer
~ Something ruinous happened here ~
yet my troughs cut a thousand tongues to sing
over scarred gneissic terrain from Toxaway Falls
and rush vibrant white down narrow slotted slides to where Twin
Falls splits over cliff face boulders all mylonitic colors
like light gold, frankincense, myrrh, black, gray shades, pink,
hues fit to praise the King. And below, my water rides
consistently wild miles of chutes, rapids, long v-shaped slides
that look from the sky like bright reed pens of ancient scribes
carving tribute through Energizer Narrows to gush Chub Line
Falls that twists pops locks over massive jagged rocks pounding
        exaltation of God
who by His favor made my rugged mountain stand strong.
So, my stubborn beauty flows comforted to Wintergreen Falls
and one last massive graceful s-curve to meet Jocassee.

4

See me: Horsepasture River, Toxaway's bubbly sister,
like the Red Sea dancer I too survived potential disaster,
parting dams on both north and south sides,
raising timbrels high 18 miles to sing with creeks after.
Hear my canticles: Mighty river am I, of dashing vigor full,
yet humble before the Creator, desperate, fervent to praise Him.
My way? Fill Lake Sapphire, then drop and pool, drop and pool,
like loud Hebrew psalmist celebration punctuated by Selah ~
when rocks stop playing and my water softly sings a cappella –
then breaks again ~ frothy over my steep riverbed of
ten thousand crystalline boulders scattered like coins in a coffer.
At Drift Falls, I ooze (across augen rock)
thick perfume from alabaster box on His feet,
and at Turtleback Falls, I fan out, oil poured down, offered
to anoint the songs of these domed stone priests.
Then lofty Rainbow Falls in many cascades to honor His name
plunge so fervently wind is raised, and mist rises incense prayer.
Sometimes sun rays join this congregation, lift bright bow on air:
visible palpable signs that His glory is there. Stunning scene,
but I pray you see Him – that's why I descend
on to Stairstep Falls ledges where pride falls level
      by level
            by level,
and where pride sinks, worship rises most effervescent:
on to fast, frenzied passion, Highway to Heaven Falls reckless
down to ineffable Windy Falls long, tall, stretching
      over multi-sectioned
cliffs hallowed out, caved in by time, but singing ceaseless
      with me to Jocassee.

5

See me: Whitewater River, 14-mile body of water
with knowledge like Old Testament prophets.
Strange and beautiful calling,
mine, to form squeezed entire through high narrow slot canyon.

Hear my lamentations: bluffs folded in over me,
pressed by desire for faithfulness, desire for justice,
gray striated rocks of schist produced by intense crushing,
by incredible pressure, shaken together,
I run from Cashiers through rocky aisles with good measure.
I run though most never see my Entrance Falls, Sculpted Falls,
my Exit Falls in the unearthly canyon of my upriver.
Most never risk the rock-climbing, trek, intense effort.
Perilous, the highest praise. Most only see when they see forever.
Yet blessed are those who trace my songs of celebration,
who understand glory of a river like the Cherokee Nation.
I feel glorious terror of the Almighty
as I plunge the precipice of 55 Mph Falls to hit my watery knees
in a huge pool, wide, smooth, still flowing reverent and deep.
Does your singing stop and leave you yet hungry
for communion, for more of His peace?
My singing, my leaping stones doesn't cease.
Rapidly pulsating sanctuary, my Sabbath lasts all week.
Joy! I cry, power and joy for sorrows accepted and overcome.
Tears of gratefulness fall unencumbered as my voice thunders:
Upper Whitewater Falls – multi-tiered high sounding cymbals.
Lower Whitewater Falls shapes whole river to mighty singular
cascade, hammering praise for His passion on rock below,
      dance and timbrel,
both great falls visible from Lake Jocassee's uplifted face.

6

And see me: Thompson River, wildest herald,
I leaped even in the womb of earth's spring,
deep in highest Sassafras Mountain beginning.
Fast and early, I rush to run 8 miles extremely steep
striated biotite rock of black or dark green mica shimmering,
in dense wilderness gorge, my urgent torrent voice crying,
Prepare ye the way of the Lord!
Hear my riotous exhortations:
in remote rocky bluff banks my cathedral,

around huge open-air stalagtites looking like steeples,
testify, ecstasy, rejoice, delight – He is the Christ!
Sharp, rugged, my way narrows:
I kiss with reverence the logs, the crossed logs
that shape my path and flow.
If they are locust logs, I am wild honey
tumbling from White Owl Falls many chutes
fling glory, glory to God in the highest,
like oil-drenched grain flung by levitical priest to altar fire,
like droplets shooting out when one rises from baptizing,
down to High Falls, then tall fervent loud voice of Big Falls cries
to remind other rivers: He descended far too
He too was poured out, spilled out, spitefully used,
so I cast myself down for Him in one last intense mile.
I was born for this, and though my end is violent,
I've been reassured by Him. I run crashing to Jocassee with
    resolute smile.

7

Four spirited rivers, how could they not shine?
From rising sun to setting again,
glory rays skim boisterous waters, spring forth
over quartz, mica, feldspar textured crystalline,
glint and glimmer in wonder of Him.
And look at any mountain creek
for microcosm of these streams:
same rapids, same sieves, slides, eddies, waves
small scale, like all rivers tiny mirrors of heaven's praise.

When Jocasssee Valley Cherokee revered going to water,
this always meant touching a river,
not a manmade lake. It was the rivers they held sacred
vital symbol of paradise found.
Motion, flow, sound of rocks cry out
as water falls – impossible without a higher place.
High praise! Beauty falls to us. It comes down.

In concert with rocks, rivers raise
songs to revere Him all night, all day.
Lively Blue Wall waters gather into one flow,
foretaste of crystal river from His throne.

In awe, Lake Jocassee must be still and know
what she knows.

Wild Honey

Of course, there are those
who will help us spin
straw into gold –
for the mere price
of our priceless souls.

So what did you
come here to see?
Some sort of shaking reed?
The mother lode
sought three, four hundred years ago
by James Moore, perhaps de Soto?
Gleaming diversity of plants
sought by Andre Michaux
in this innocent valley
destined to be
transformed so radically?
A shimmering creek
where sun rays dance
into your trembling dusty cup,
glowing, Kabbalistic liquid,
secret missing piece
that completes
your lifelong efforts at alchemy?

Shin-deep you stand
next to your craft
where this mountain lake
expands out like hope
that you can live again
the morning after
your soul's blackest night.
The joy of possibility:
not knowing what
you, on your water venture,
will find.

Hopefully insight –
Hopefully the fountain of life,
   the philosopher's stone –
Hopefully you'll see yourself
simply mesmerized
by this thick gold:
Pollen
sprinkled lavishly
on a sanctified
rippling cove
by infinitely wise
old munificent pines.

Jocassee's Green Bird

I look across shards of untranslatable time.
Not a princess, not a lost one,
I know who and where I am. Do you see me?
I stand to the west at the edge of uweyv
watching water fall from the eyes of the hills.
I have no tears left.
I raise my arms in the broken morning
and call for him, singing We n' de ya ho.

I see the green bird, Carolina parakeet,
flying to me from Old Eastatoee
over the divide.
He wears the sun on his head.
He lands on my outstretched hand.
His feet circle my ring finger.
We sing together with leaves on the breeze
as I hold him to my breast, We n' de ya ho.

Cosmic Storm

Time seems eerily still
as I awake from reverie
drifting in my kayak
where Whitewater River
meets Lake Jocassee at Bad Creek.
Motor boats I've seen
fifteen (or thirty?) minutes ago
have vanished
like spirits heading for another world.
My eyes widen with horror
at a massive, inky black thunderhead
that now obscures all light
over an unseen boat ramp miles south.
I find myself alone.

Frantically, I turn the boat
toward this approaching Charybdis of a storm
and begin to paddle straight her way.
This water has changed identity
from serene sister to gnarly Scylla,
with each rolling wave on surface
now a snaky knot
in strands of her liquid hair.
Air becomes cooler
as a contentious wind
stings skin on my face and arms.
Fiercely, I set my jaw
and stroke toward the distant ramp.

My head now highest
point on the water,
I wonder – should I pull to shore
and get off this massive
sheet of mineral
electrical conductivity?
Then I realize tree limbs
are waving a collective No
to show me that waves
will turn me over
as they slap steep land,
and if this frazzled lake
doesn't pull me under,
lightning will shock
tallest sheltering pine,
set woods on fire,
and spin the wind through,
forcing branches into bobbing and thrusting each other
in a dance of dangerous arboreal swordplay.
I know all this in a flash
of spiritually-charged insight.

Jerking with a start at the first bang of thunder,
(Count to five,
How close is it?
I can't remember!)
Two miles turn to twenty
as I stroke on liquid treadmill
getting nowhere while angels
war the atmosphere around me.
With superhuman speed, born of terror,
I finally approach the dock,
just now seeing first dreaded bolt
of serrated light over Devil's Fork
and feeling first drops of storm
tap my skin like they have something to tell me.

My boat touches shore,
but the moment my foot meets land,
Satan must have insulted Gabriel again
(Milton's *Paradise Lost* - Book IV, it's on)
because gusts sweep sand
and blast my face, my body, my kayak,
and pelt the few hazy men still trying
to tie dripping boats in trailers.
Intensifying raindrops
become tiny projectiles on the gale.
With no time to kiss ground,
I take shelter where I'm found
to watch the mighty show
of light and sound and fluid energy.

Sometimes angels
make Jocassee their combat zone.
Who knows why.
Lust for conquest did not start with us.
Maybe loveliest Edens remain
most prone to nastiest contention
among supernatural powers.
Whatever the reason,
I'm grateful for the full experience,
quickened ~ invigorated to drift
more consciously another day,
where I've escaped harm,
unstruck by crossfire
of the cosmic storm.

Umbrella Sailing

In excitement of a trip,
going always seems
much shorter than coming back,
and here, this phenomenon's
compounded by regular southwest winds
sweeping across afternoons
requiring extra thrust
of spent bodies
paddling return voyages
from anywhere on this lake.

So, favorable moment
that finds you, seven o'clock,
rowing breakneck to beat the dark
when rare northeast wind turns from heaven
cooling your back! If you find yourself blessed
with such lucky stroke,
open up your umbrella for sail, turn paddle to rudder,
and enjoy being
moved, pulled steadily to harbor
by something worlds above your own power.

Wright Creek Bluegrass

Things change when a body brings
a banjo out and makes it ring ~
rousing shrill staccato notes
jangling clanking upbeat souls:

Cl~ink Clink Clink Clink Clink Clink
Cla~ng, Cla~ng, Clink Clink Clink!
Cla~ng, Cla~ng, Cla~ng, Clink
Cla~ng, Cla~ng, Clink Clink Clink!

Things change when a cloudburst sky
floods this mountain's western side ~
Wright Creek splashes sparkling bright,
hammers boulders, licks, and slides:

Cla~ng, Cla~ng, Cla~ng, Clink
Cla~ng, Cla~ng, Clink Clink Clink!
Cla~ng, Cla~ng, Cla~ng, Clink
Cla~ng, Cla~ng, Clink Clink Clink!

C~areful, or you'll miss the sound
which round the cove resonates loud:
Water rolls arpeggios ~
Nature's got her Gold Tone out!

Cla~ng, Cla~ng, Cla~ng, Clink
Cla~ng, Cla~ng, Clink Clink Clink!
Cla~ng, Cla~ng, Cla~ng, Clink
Cla~ng, Cla~ng, Clink Clink Clink!

Neck of rooted maple trees,
God's hand plucks each liquid string ~
Lovely cascades drop in threes:
Wright Creek Falls plays Cripple Creek ~

Cl~ink Clink Clink Clink Clink Clink Clink
Cla~ng, Cla~ng, Clink Clink Clink!
Cla~ng, Cla~ng, Cla~ng, Clink
Cla~ng, Cla~ng, Clink Clink Clink!

Jesus needs no plastic picks ~
Mighty fine high droplets pitch ~
Foggy mountain fifth-string drone,
water's rhythmic brightness glows:

Cla~ng, Cla~ng, Cla~ng, Clink
Cla~ng, Cla~ng, Clink Clink Clink!
Cla~ng, Cla~ng, Cla~ng, Clink
Cla~ng, Cla~ng, Clink Clink Clink!

Banjo head with rocky rim,
ice brook splash to face again ~
Clog-dance here with muddy feet,
Wright Creek Falls plays Cripple Creek!

Cl~ink Clink Clink Clink Clink Clink Clink
Cla~ng, Cla~ng, Clink Clink Clink!
Cla~ng, Cla~ng, Cla~ng, Clink
Cla~ng, Cla~ng, Clink Clink Clink!

Float with ghosts behind the strings ~
Wright Creek Falls plays Cripple Creek!
Cla~ng, Cla~ng, Cla~ng, Clink ~
Clang, Clang, C~Clang, Clang ~ Clink Clink!

Variations on a Twinkle
for Emily and Sara

There's always someone to tell you
that stars don't actually twinkle,
and you might one day know, they're right –
that it's just cosmic mist intermittently
obscuring the view –
but I hope you'll choose to usually refuse
to believe it, really.

Because you're constantly finding
a dozen new ways
to play that old twinkle diddy
on shining fiddles.
For you, stars still sparkle – stellarly.
Sometimes, refusing to believe
is the brightest thing, little stars.

It's true with stars and with tunes, too:
They twinkle if they twinkle to you.

Eastern Phoebe at Horsepasture River
Northeast Jocassee

perched on her branch
just above the stream
of consciousness,
this eastern phoebe stands
almost as still as the hour
before sunrise.

she bobs her tail
like rhythm of a beating heart.

over the rapid
thoughts buzz by like gnats;
the phoebe flies to catch
one – leaving her perch,
snatching the midge,
landing fast again on her ledge.

feeding, she circles in the wind –
to honor the path of the sun.

Homeowners

Warblers, wild creatures of Fishers Knob property,
build on 3.1 million dollar acres for free:
no mortgage, no taxes, no hoa fees.

Shine

Twelve mile circle,
six thousand strokes
to arrive where I began –
this boat ramp at this moment
where a certain slant
of light on lake water
still as glass
drew my eyes upward
to this unwalled open clerestory,
nature's twilight mass.

I stood wading with
a sister I'd just met
waiting for the strength
to leave this place
when instantly seven tree swallows appeared
(Did they fly here?)
wearing Abbot Suger's stained glass
on their shining iridescent backs
mystery of metallic green blue purple
all in one. They stole my breath.

Strange thing, friends of Francis,
they didn't sing
but with short, sharp notes
insisted attention to "This! This!"
What cosmic power in soft small wings
that with each ecstatic pass
brushed away the veil
of material mass
that's been scribbled over truth
by millennia of misguided pursuits.

Then dabbing eager feet
in last shimmering light of day
(their ink), turning and cutting
they etched luminous letters on cobalt sky,
reflected on the water
in calligraphy long-forgotten by us.
The words were foreign
but I've known their lucid meaning forever.
At the heart of the Book of Nature is
the one glistening Word: all words for shine in one.

The birds will remain with me,
like an afterimage behind the eyelids
from staring intently at something brilliant.
Afterglow of sublime incandescent violet blue green
on top of their wings
lingers, and I've seen in these
but lower, shorter wavelength sheens
in the visible spectrum –
not highest, longest waves that
emanate color of consuming fire above.

Ancient Call

Sooner or later,
if you kayak still water long enough,
it will happen to you.
Two damselflies in the act of –
reproduction…. will land locked together
in their mobile, winged wheel
of copulative embrace,
on your arm,
on your leg!
At first, it will feel –
improper, somewhat voyeuristic,
as if you intrude
the proverbial boudoir of these
flying jewels.
But you need to see them.
It's life-changing.
Worldwide, they carry the gospel of let there be light
(and let there be life)
in twenty billion sentient,
benevolent kind of curious eyes.
Without such light, there is no life.
In a dramatic display of moving love,
these insects literalize
our conception of this act.
Hold each other close;
Perch on the edge of the inner drive –
The moment comes together just right:
We soar, we fly, and light makes life!
So, bless these little marvels
and what they share with you,
elemental sign of an ancient call:
Be fruitful, and multiply!

Testify!

So this is the life!
Even in frigid reaches,
a globe, capped and cradled
by frozen beaches,
Consecrated –
Emperor penguins warm in Arctic huddles,
Polar bears learn to hunt with their mothers,
Belugas and bearded seals dive under
ten-feet ice shelves,
joining narwhals, humpback, and bowhead whales
sustained by super virile – tiny – krill.
Hundreds of feet below Antarctic freeze,
in salt water, still liquid at 29 degrees,
Thrive (Thrill!)
bioluminescent jellyfish, sea anemones,
swimming feather stars' delicate yellow, blue-green
palm-frond arms, citrine-colored sea squirts,
and foot-wide mustard spiders marine!
So much gold, so much glow
would exist here
though we were snowblind
though we didn't know
(whether we ever saw).
What is this
– Life –
These dynamos
that break the ice?
Fruit of the indomitable drive
of survival's will?
Tenacious! Exquisite!

And the whole earth is filled with...

Preach, oh, preach!
Testify!

So this is the life!
Even in scorching ranges,
a planet, heated, highlighted
by sand dune paintings,
Hallowed –
Wrens and elf owls inhabit holes in cactus,
Beetles flip fog droplets off their own backs – survival tactic –
Two-humped camels thrive Gobi extremes,
green mirage, occasional waking dream.
Roadrunners (gritty birds!) eat rattlesnakes
then leave predators dazed with x-shaped tracks,
horned lizards, wild asses, high plateau yaks,
caracals and small burrowing desert sand cats.
On virtually no rain per year,
shivering nights, hundred-degree days that sear,
Survive (Surprise!)
antelope oryxs crowned with black spears,
jackals and jack rabbits extravagant ears,
hardy 700-year-old boojum tree
branches lift cryptic letters on Baja breeze:
Words summer hummers know how to read!
So much bloom, so much beauty
would persist here
though we were sandstorm blind
though we didn't see
(whether we ever perceived)
What is this
– Life –
These prize fighters
that drink it dry?
Open and naked in most parched of places
living oasis on soil baked with blazes?
Clay jars
filled with antithesis of death,
Filled with breath?
Steadfast! Blessed!

….with His glory

Preach, oh, preach!
Testify!

So this is the life!
And at Jocassee, the living is easy,
a lake stemming from, sustained
by five gorgeous streams –
Sanctified!
Four hundred-pound black bears sleep high hollow trees
or dig dens red clay covered with leaves,
teaching cubs blind and bald, as soon as they see
to take their pick of buds and berries
oak acorns, pine nuts, and a bit of meat
especially grubs and yellow jacket bees.
Such zing
in this temperate Eden rich with mammals' milk and honey
watched by barred owls, great horned owls, little owls screech.
Rough-winged swallows shore bank burrow 2-4 feet deep,
woodpeckers, sand plovers, warblers, and geese,
wild turkeys prosper on blooming wild weeds.
Then also here in this waterful place
graced by phytoplankton rich lake summer 75 degrees
and four distinct seasons from winter to spring,
Breathe (Breathtaking!)
bluegill, bass, rainbow, brown trout, carp,
belted kingfishers, bald eagles, hawks,
great herons, hummingbirds, deer, feral hogs,
peregrine falcons at Jumping Off Rock,
ospreys, otters, spring peeper tree frogs,
loons sublime call on waves of night,
prismal dragonflies, damselflies glint daylight.
Songbirds sing over gneissic streams,
world's most diverse salamanders,
broadhead, blue-tailed skinks.
And those mammals – raccoons, skunks,

coyotes, bobcats, cougars (yes, I believe),
ground squirrels, gray squirrels, otters, and minks.
So much zest, so much blaze
would flourish here
though we were sun-stare blind
though we never gazed
(whether we were ever amazed)
What is this
– Life –
These perpetually young
that suck endless earth marrow supply?
This vivaciousness
in vessels of flesh?
They sun and nurse here
amid Oconee bells, honeysuckle, muscadine vines,
ferns, mountain laurel, rhodedenron,
pitch, white, scrub, shortleaf pines,
old-growth forest, dogwood tree blooms,
wildflowers lush.
Have you seen them?
Or are they rare in your life as the sight
of Greenland's walrus
or Sonoran sandfish?

Bodies and faces
playing in one of the last pristine places,
complex vibrant power plant machines
with plenty to eat,
and room for speed?
Created! Satiated!
No wonder life
Lives (Look!)
in this place with little lack
where horned grebe chicks
cross lake on parents' backs.
Hosts of species
mating and eating
moving (growing)

dashing, animated, effervescent, leaping,
copious, lavish, sacred, learning, and breathing.

Ordained! Spirited! Teeming!

Surely there is a Great Back
that carries,
ferries
all of life
across the span
of a watery
universe crackling with nourishment
whether fecund, frozen, or fiery.

Seeing –
Fully seeing –
Creatures
as they're just Being,
as they find daily means
of gaining Energy under the sun,
will make you
Yourself
Wander (Wonder!)
Exist (Exclaim!)
perpetually
Aware
Alive
Glad of the breath in you
and wondering at its source

Let everything that has breath....

Preach, oh, preach!
Testify!

water in the air
humidity palpable
red hawk swims through sky

Jumping Off Rock

Is there water in the air?
Do birds swim in it?
Something in me is
desperate to fly.
Perched on the crag
of Jumping Off Rock,
how many years
has it hesitated,
asking, "jumping off – into what?"
yet eager to leave this bough
and soar in pure jubilant freedom
dropping off every pain
and fear
like feathers off wings –
feathers that gently
lilt on open air
down to lake
here with its horseshoe shape,
riding boat after boat's wake
through warm drifting days
across the spillway
down to Lake Keowee
and maybe a year later
far down to Keowee River
where it drifts
on Little River
there picked up
by an osprey
to soften a nest
for her brood.
At least a dozen times

this flight-worthy thing in me has asked,
heart quickening,
muscles tensing,
feeling a mighty pull
skyward,
Is it now? –
Is it now? –
But it's impossible to fly
and clutch a familiar ledge.

Carpe Diem

I see the carp swimming
long and striated below me
with unaffected grace
but today I've neither muster nor mettle
to leap this swimming hole rock
into the cool nurturing lake.

Expanding Range

I can hardly believe –
but flashes of white edges
on massive eagle feathers
cross widest water
to land on highest reach
of scrubby pine
right before my eyes.
"Look!" I cry
to a boy of thirteen
who just pulled his
inflatable raft
next to me.
Quick glance,
stretch of his neck,
chuckled breath released,
then he says, "That's not real."
Wry grin, and he adds, "Park rangers
probably hung that fake thing."
Young cynic, yet such vast energy,
but then, the resilient, adaptable young
always take it well.

And to you –
What is real?
Open water to hunt,
fish to fill stomach's creel?
Yellow eyes that see slightest
motion in field?
Pliability beyond
what must have baffled
your great grandparents:
mystery of eggs
that never hatched.
They nudged them over and over
with bright beaks
then moved on,

expanding range
with survival's call,
will incontestable as steel.
You don't have to believe it to see.
You don't have to sing
with incredible range
or delight us
with sweet-natured habits
to make us believe
Life's driving force can heal.

Let beauty, vision, faith fan out
~ feathers on eight-foot wings ~
full, unpretentious flight.

Lift Up the Serpent

And there he is – the wise and crooked serpent,
not in the fall, but in the beginning –
right there among the creeping things
creeping on earth,
right there among what God pronounces good,
though things have not gone well for him.

Today I pray to see Jocassee wild,
some new astounding sight of creatures loving life.
Five minutes, and I rise to take my boat.
Then, right there among what God pronounces good,
this orange-patterned snake with fluid grace
comes swimming yard-long by my feet,
five-inch fish in his fang-filled mouth.
I freeze ~ He makes perfect s-curves on the lake.

So there I am – my prayer being answered,
not swimming bear, rooting boar, frolicking otter,
but water snake feasting on bluegill fresh food
right there among what God pronounces good.
Glad – one day, lions will eat straw, and snakes will eat dirt
and babies will play next to den of snakes' brood.

Rattled
Rattlesnake Joe

Thirsty for the wild,
I drink the sight of you,
timber rattlesnake,
as you swim toward shore
near Mill Creek Fall's bank ~
such jolting grace!

Best cup of coffee I Ever Had,
perfect blend ~
splotches across your back
alternating patches
cream-and-sugar tan
and pine tar pitch
black.
All-natural stimulant
living dash of cinnamon
stripe down your spine ~
and mine! Aromatic spirit
born of dark gum rosin and turpentine.

From my kayak
seeing you swim holding your face
and rattle tip out of the lake,
I never felt so awake.
Never knew what life meant.
Never knew!

You're certainly an earthy brew,
strong, full-bodied, woody,
notes of scrub bark and wintergreen
over pitch pine nuts infused.
You taste like pure robusta beans.
No way to sip you slowly
or daintily

like a sugar cookie latte,
your presence had to be
a chug of espresso,
just laced with – dark chocolate?
Maple syrup? Black walnut?

And though I won't be taking your tail
like a mug handle any time soon,
alert and alive
I've shed caffeine jitters
for consistently stirring,
piquantly biting memory of you

Double Springs Harmonic: How It's Done

How many times I've forced myself
to load my boat and leave
this lake at twilight
before the symphony
is even half-begun.
Strange new feeling, then:
rowing out
toward Double Springs
to camp tonight
(to stay the night!)
in Jocassee woods.
Eager to encounter
the lake's mood in darkness,
we place our tent
and hear water
kiss ground with waves
gently insistent
like mother spoons her infant
his first whole food.

Soon, though, more campers arrive
in the hall of the mountain king:
eighteen adolescent
embodiments of kinetic energy
exploding air and water.
Nightfall comes
and we wonder
how this masculine movement
can rest comfortably distributed
in just three tents.
A few more hours of agitato ensue,
"Man, please, can't you move?"
loud olfactory remnants of greasy food,
"Get off me, Dude!"
and raucous laughter unsubdued.

After midnight, in relative quiet,
one boy cleverly sets off
a cadenza of teen tenors
mimicking owl whooooos
for roughly three hours.

Finally, when this place seems to sigh
that our innocents have exhausted
themselves to sleep,
fermata on terra firma,
the real owls begin to play
their ancient notes –
a music carried far and clear
on still, cool black air.
A screech owl, watching
just above us all night long:
violin of Novacek's Perpetuum Mobile,
now whirrs high-pitched trill,
his whole body a vibrating thrill.
A barred owl deeper
up Thompson River replies
barking four, then five notes at a time
in fuller-throated tone:
bassoon of Mozart's Concerto,
b flat major. Then the loons,
trumpeters of Horsepasture Side,
Musterground Mountain,
play quivering arrangement of taps to honor
the passing of delicious dark.
That's how it's done, boys,
That's how it's done.

Whistling: A Handbook
(Inspired by a lifetime of whistling and a day of paddling Jocassee while whistling Tracy Chapman's First Person on Earth*)*

Welcome
So you want to be a whistler?
What a windfall! It's likely you didn't find whistling
but this ancient art and practice found you
who heard its magnetic call
like a sheep drawn out of the hazy hills of Ephraim
by the captivating, piercing tone
of your shepherd –
aural flag that your ears recognized
hoisted in homeward blue.
Most often, a true whistler is born, not forced or formed.

When birds eat seeds, the possibilities
of what all those seeds would have become
settle into their souls.
That is why they whistle.
They don't choose it –
it's a compulsion they cannot resist.
And why would they?
Listen to a goldfinch:
You'll hear the bright notes of sunflowers and mostly thistle.
Listen to a rose-breasted grosbeak:
You'll hear a sun-kissed berry digested
come back out the beak
and ripen into music on the air –
sweet, juicy notes pulled down by acoustic gravity
one by one in vigorous, satiated trickle.
So that's what a fresh wild blueberry sounds like!

Why Whistle?
You are about to open a window to elemental tradition
extending from earliest humans to postmodern cyborgs,
from creek bank to concert hall.
Whistling is natural.
Ever since first human shelter,
we have heard wind whistle across the air,
its momentum split by our walls in its way.
Earth itself has always whistled
in consensual harmony with the wind:
searing Sahara sands, or screaming Everest's jet stream,
from Rockies down turning shrill speed cross Tornado Alley
over Mount Washington northeast out to sea,
and sometimes shrieking across Jocassee
to push up waves four or five feet.
In fact, whistling gales must have been integral
in beginning the very beginning,
when the Spirit moved with such dynamic speed
across the face of the waters
that the animating energy of that singing, singeing sound
opened up the space for light to become Day.
That Holy Wind has never grown winded,
and a generous portion of that inspired cosmic gust
has been placed in us.

Whistling ability gifts us with musical instrument
transported within at all times
in every location, indoors, outdoors,
at the desk, on the lake,
and with proper training
there's no need
for tuning or regular maintenance.
Storage space, carrying case? You. All natural you.

As old as human beings,
whistling often comes out of us unwittingly,
kettle of boiling water with escaping steam,

force of expression to voice what we mean –
the noise "whew" flows out when overcome with wonder
at something we hardly believe,
fans of a homerun, to cheer the team.
In some countries, it screeches the boo of soccer mob,
or the "whoot-whew" when we're turned on –
It's in our genes.

Whistling, most unencumbered of musical arts,
unbelabored, unpretentious technique,
requires such economy of means.
Mini grand piano? Twenty five hundred dollars.
Acoustic guitar? Divide that by five.
Beginner saxophone? Three hundred and two.
Student flute? One twenty three.
Whistle? Free –
with the price of expending breath across teeth.
(If you like, you can use a blade of grass.
They freely cover the earth).
A whistler's instrument
is virtually indestructible.
In fact, wetting your whistle
will make it function best.

Two people group nations
communicate through language
of whistled articulations,
but most practitioners use whistling
just for certain situations:
setting our minds on a morning song,
closing a productive day,
family tradition, carried on,
amusement through a boring job,
catharsis of an aching wrong,
signal that we'd rather not talk,
calm for nerves and fears of the dark.
Some (Anna Leonowens style) whistle to act as though

they're not afraid,
and find one day, they're not.

There is a music in the human spirit
undaunted by depression,
unfettered by torture,
unconquered by death.
In the great stories, long, reiterated
insistent whistles of trains
evoke inevitability of pain,
or, more wondrously – of joy.

Getting Started (Basic Techniques to Begin)
If your goal is attention-grabbing, crowd-silencing,
athlete-pacing, alarm-sounding, or thief-halting,
the two-finger method is your style,
(a human whistle can be heard six tenths of a mile)
giving the ear-piercing effect
of coach, referee, or police whistle
(also used by country parents in lieu of dinner bells,
by hunters summoning wild game,
and by worldwide canine owners calling in best friends).
Yet the more sophisticated method emphasized here
aims for music and ends in melodies
that rival Carolina mockingbirds, whistling virtuosos
who embody dawn and join the song
of McKinneys Creek (and all the cadenced creeks)
warbling easy and unburdened about this lake.

If you have breath, lips, tongue, teeth, palate, larynx, and chin,
you have the components to the human whistle,
your own ever-present resonance chamber
of latent potential –
but it may come as bad news: the complex sound production
process which comes more naturally to some
proves somewhat mysterious.

The One who placed music in the spheres
and sings over us lovingly
created us with a built-in woodwind
and to play it, the lips must be positioned
halfway between
resting posture of silence
and pursed stance taken when
poised for a kiss.
The closest parallel with speech would be this:
place your lips as if about to say the approximant
w that begins the word why or whistle itself.
Next, summon breath from within
and blow gliding out across lips
in w position.
If you only get hollow sound,
you need very subtle tightening lips
and facial muscles that surround,
and to engage air through larynx
for rich tone – but where does this tone come from?
(It certainly isn't a vocal cord hum).
You should find your tongue raised
toward your soft palate,
and when you sound lower notes,
your tongue's farther back,
but move through higher range,
tongue's progressively closer
to front of mouth,
touching back of lower teeth
at highest note you reach.
It's your flute within –
your tongue the means of closing the virtual holes:
tongue moves forward;
air waves shorten,
producing higher notes.

Don't be discouraged early on.
Pretty soon, you'll be doing a Charlie Parker,

a Dizzy Gillespie, you know –
You'll forget all this and just blow.
Blow out and breath
gives voice to a tune
already there on the air,
like Whistler the painter
brushing on colors layer after layer
freeing images too long
hidden in canvas fibers.

For the Advanced
Whistling fills emptiness with music,
like filling the air with tiny shape-note lights
to replace fireflies
that vanished from a field just paved.
When the birds stop their singing to hear you,
you'll know you've arrived.
To test how your skill has progressed,
give this a try:
one Jocassee morning, with sun
still fairly low in sky,
put your kayak on water
and bear to northwest side
up Devil's Fork arm,
past the massive, solitary mansion
where water's still wide.
At this point, begin to whistle
something lilting and slow,
(Tracy Chapman's First Person on Earth
or Beethoven's Für Elise will do).
Now, row as far as you can go
up narrowing headwaters
until you see that petite whistling legend
of a bird, the eastern wood pewee
perched directly above river
on her hangout branch of tree.

It's her whistling stage –
She'll be there. You'll see.
If by now she has not flown away
but has stopped her aubade
to hear yours, cocking her tiny head,
you may count yourself
a whistler of God.

Who's Who (Learning from Sounds like Sweet Georgia Brown)
As you journey to such an accomplished place,
take inspiration from the greats,
finding their familiar moods and tunes
became a subconscious part of you
long ago – in your psyche like
numbers, colors, shapes.
Popular singers have found whistling
perfect accent to vocal style, tone,
theme, and lyrics of songs.
You should know Adriana Caselotti's Whistle While You Work,
though the song (filled with bells and whistles)
contains only very brief pure human samples.
For more distinct flair, see John O'Neill's prominent trill
in The Good, Bad, and Ugly Theme,
iconic highlight of Western film,
evoking rattlesnakes striking rolling tumbleweeds.
Then check out John Sebastian whistling
up a Lovin Spoonful of carefree in Day Dream.
And although Guy Mitchell excels
at Singing the Blues,
his shrill whistling best expresses
deep things he stood to lose.
Masterful Otis Redding's closing warble
highlights his mellow ode
to lethargy in Dock of the Bay.
Rock band Scorpions's whistle sounds melancholy
longing for peace to waft in on Wind of Change.

And with Nile mystique, the Bangles's
Susanna Hoffs memorably whistles
listeners into a merry trancelike state
of Walking Like an Egyptian.
In fact, whistlers find a watershed in the 80s:
A melodic, slow whistle drag is just made
for Axl Rose's invocation to patience.
Bobby McFerrin, chipper, tweets "Don't Worry,"
and soon multiple harmonizing whistles
indeed signal happy places.
Pat Benatar's mournful whistle
serves perfect coda to memorialize
Cupid-slain casualties of love's battlefield.
Mark Snow's hauntingly warbled X-Files theme
voices all of us who with Mulder want to believe.
Post 2000, rock band Foster the People
adds eerily casual whistling accent
to Pumped Up Kicks to depict
cultural DNA: gun violence ever-present,
      unsurprising, expected.
And in a theme not altogether unconnected,
Peter Bjorn and John whistle to show
Young Folks longing for relationship,
unconditional love, acceptance.

For other musicians, whistling goes beyond
supporting cast to starring role.
Brother Bones' Sweet Georgia Brown must be heard.
And don't miss number one essential "Fishin Hole,"
forever linked with Andy, Mayberry;
Writer Earle Hagin whistles it so perfectly,
most wouldn't guess the song actually has words.
Professional whistlers: Sophie Tucker 1920s Yiddish vaudeville,
Geert Chatrou, NC Whistlers Champion International,
Steve Herbst (3 octave range), Carole A. Kaufman concert hall,
Jack Cohen, classical orchestral whistler of Montreal,
jazz warbler Ron McCroby, Fred Lowery, or Ronnie Ronalde,
prove their human mouth's ability serious instrument musical.

In recorded practice, whistling reached all-time 1920s-30s high,
declined post-war 1940-70, leveled off
mid-song, John Lennon's 1971 Jealous Guy,
in 80s popular music, revived,
then another cultural increase around 2000.
Who knows why?
But we're glad to find whistling on the rise.

All of the above greats have been fairly recent in time,
Thus, such a collection stands inevitably incomplete.
Millenia ago, what unrecorded whistled musical feats
echoed over Viking sea, African game trail,
Native American council, or Scottish highland,
across every continent?
Maybe they performed a sort of whistling unknown
       to postmodern man.
Maybe one day soon, we'll learn it again.

A Final Word on What to Expect
Even if you reach the skill of Geert Chatrou,
some will find your practice annoying
and wish to silence or banish you
to swinging a pickaxe forever underground
if you refuse to shortly pipe down.
Perhaps afflicted with barrenness of spirit
or untutored in proper frequency to hear it,
either way, pray for those
who disdain the magical sound,
but while you're praying,
give them a break –
or they'll deem you obnoxious
and may never come round.
Let's hope, too, that we've moved past
centuries when some found
the practice improper,

particularly for those of female gender
(Thank heaven for Jo guiding Little Women).

Hearing a different vibe,
my cat draws near when I whistle but can't seem to decide
if she loves it or loathes it, if pleasure or pain.
When whistling begins,
she finds my lap and gets close as she can
but my scars prove her response
when high register gives her ears strain.
Perhaps she instinctively senses power in the craft
and resists becoming the Pied Piper of Hamelin's rats.

For centuries, sailors have seen capacity
of whistler's skill to draw in
wind to fill sails again
to propel mission forward
days and nights on end.
Careful where and how you use such power!
You could summon wild animals
enamored with the reverberations.
There are cultures, perhaps rightly,
who do not take this force of whistling lightly.
Russians and Romanians have feared to whistle inside
fearing the sound would lead to economic blight.
Estonians believe such jangling whirs could set your house afire.
And beware the time:
Some refuse to whistle like owls at night
fearing evil is attracted to the noise,
and British superstition claims
The Seven Whistlers call out prophecies
of death or calamity that destroys.

Isaiah says The God of Justice
will whistle in plagues of flies and bees
and in the end whistle for nations

to come together across vast contentious seas,
The Great Shepherd whistling for his scattered sheep.
After Auschwitz, a young Jewish boy could hardly believe
the tune he heard through hospital din –
his grandfather whistling their family's song.
Thus, he found him – reunited again.
And if you're fortunate enough
to have had a whistling father,
maybe this is how you'll find your daddy
in the vastness of heaven?
The jaunty, whistled sound of his song
(for mine, "Down Yonder" or "The Entertainer")
will come lilting on pure unencumbered ethereal air
from his direction.
That whistle is how you'll know he's there;
That whistle is how you'll know where.

One day, Gabriel will sound
the all-conclusive, universal five o'clock whistle,
and weary work days for all of time will be done.
How fortunate the whistlers – who found this musical
transitional object that bridged them from here
to unfathomable new music of eternal home.

Everything

lines just to say
seven (and seventy) years
of looking at this place
learning, nursing
(drinking all in)
didn't mean a thing
But everything.

white-tailed mother deer
her cautious eye
on the way
her speckled fawn licked and played
nursed and drank
meant nothing
But everything.

Mother of All Theories

If there is a theory of everything,
the answer must be largely maternal in nature.
Isn't this a giant uterus, this fecund universe,
whose plasma generates just-right chemical balance?
Fluid, mother country surrounds,
nourishes, nurtures each of us,
keeps us warm like fetuses
amid cosmic stem cells cushioning Earth?

In creatures, the substance
doesn't disappear with a birth!
Water breaks –
Amniotic liquid

morphs to metaphysical
invisible
spiritual fortitude
constant vibrating pulse
constitutes a mother's identity.
In her universe, one major chorus
encompasses every verse:
My baby will survive, my child will thrive!
Strong as gravity, nuclear, or electromagnetic forces,
this fervently tender drive.

Fifteen, and you blushed
to hear her love you to the moon and back,
but what if this adoration, this agape, *IS*
the same as the lunar force that
pulls tides to and from the beach,
that charges protons with electricity,
or holds H_2O together, universal problem solvent
of comfort and stability,
guides birds as they migrate magnetically,
allows water strider to walk on lake surface
as if it has higher viscosity,
grounds us all with security of gravity?
And if you try to split Mama from her baby
will you not find a nuclear reaction
against your person
that would leave you to question
all you thought you knew
of cosmic explosion or fission?
Attempting such division
would be a dark, dark matter
for you, indeed.
Coming between black bear and her cub?
Rue the decision.

Motherly love,
comprised of steadfast, crackling stuff:
deep-seated, vital, elemental

secret, universe's cup.
Original, it originates.
The womb the hold
for all sentient living cargo,
the mother's body
stretched in gestation,
torn in birthing,
resiliently healed,
yet compelled by nature
to persistent perilous selflessness
that holds her own –
protective ozone
absorbs scorching radiation
but allows us to breathe,
heat for warmth,
and plants to eat.
Even this Earth that we're on
would be shortly destroyed
by comets, by asteroids
if not fenced and shielded
cradled amid gas giant planets
like Jupiter and Saturn
that deflect these threats
or take direct hits themselves.
Constantly ripped and burned,
they defend us well.

South of Jocassee,
fierce, spiny softshell turtle
depositing eggs in Little River
uterine mud near Newry Dam,
she will not be moved
until emptied
of two score round pinkish
treasure chests of turtle potential.
Laboriously,
she covers them with earth,

then scratches a patch
away from them to divert
predators from covert place
of special dirt.

Soft, soft, and sweet
how the yellow warbler
nestles her chicks
in bed of moss and tender leaves
over Howard Creek
that feeds the lake.
And any kingfisher, prone to flee
immediately,
will fly in place all day
on wings that burn and ache
guarding nestlings
laid deep in a hole she bored
six feet into this lake's bank.

The peregrine falcon
who ventures to attack
osprey's nest below Jumping Off Rock
finds that mother flattening her body,
feathers outspread over nestlings.
Falcon's second pass
meets osprey standing up on nest,
neck feathers prickled
hitting attacker with beak and wings
making herself large
stalwart force of will, vast,
valiant as Wallace or Spartacus
willing to be pecked
and wrestled plunging
in piercing talons, wing over wing
to bloody death.
The mother's reaction
would have varied none

had Lucifer himself
come flying over knarly ledge.
Soft warmth of nativity
turns white hot under threat,
small scale replication
of radioactive particles spinning
from fission in nuclear plant.
Who holds the sword
that pierced Mother Mary
soul and heart?

I'd stake my life on this hypothesis:
Maternal attachment bears all
that is fierce and holy,
born of raw material
indestructible
from the One who longed
to nestle Jerusalem like a hen
gathers her chicks.
Visible image of the invisible,
before anything,
He exists,
Power that holds totality
and refuge in shadow of his wings.
Deliverer who makes us born again,
force infused into mothers,
touch of Almighty sustainer,
maintainer,
adhesive of everything
from nucleus to supergiant elliptical galaxy,
brilliant, tenacious, unwavering,
formidable, indomitable,
eternal –
Love.

Precipitation 100%

What precipitated this kingfisher's violent dive
to snatch and devour the bass
under a rain-soaked sky?

Ducks in a Row

This year, a dozen Jocassee waterfowl imprinted on me
to such a degree, I had to be cruel to make them stay behind.
Early August, I ran down the beach, clapped hands and screamed
"Get back! I have to go!". Tilting their heads at me bemusedly,
they waddled into the water and swam north against the current.
Summer gone, I cried my way home.

Yet from my office seat, I now see two of them
foraging the university quad with wagging tails.
How did they find me here, forty miles away,
longing for splash landing, willing to take grass puddle for lake?
Divided flock, two I suspect still swim by loons at Musterground

And one missing altogether –
meat on someone's table, I'm afraid, never to fly again.
To save him, I would have evaded this job – bowed out. Almost.
There's a row in my mind. I disagree with myself.

Probably, four are resting in woods in the cove
with the pond off the main lake where I used to row
single-minded and content.

But the course of true love never did run smooth:
To love is to open one's self to such a fray, a row –

And the rest have flown south for all I know.

Trilocation
August 21, 2017

"I saw Isidore plowing the fields of Juan de Vargas
at sixth hour of morning, before sunrise under misty sky,"
said the priest to his comrade as they shared bread midday
at the Church of San Andrés.
"Impossible!" his friend replied,
"Isidore himself was knelt at the altar in prayer
 today at that very same moment just before dawn!"

And Saint Paul told Corinthians
hungry for transcendence,
"I was caught up to third heaven, to paradise,
to hear unspeakable words, forbidden to utter"
outside Yahweh's immediate presence.
So Paul was here. While he was there.
He didn't claim to understand it.

In this light, you may say my triple location
bears less noble motivation,
but today I saw through eclipse glasses darkly
moon pass in front of sun
over my home in Southern Appalachians.
Realizing too late full wonder of midday darkness
totality wouldn't fall here – Staying, I went to Salem:

(Salem, South Carolina, not Massachusetts)
and gasped to see two-minute-black-nightfall blanket Jocassee,
heard nature hush, frogs, birds holy awed silent at lunar shadow,
applauded with kindred souls high on Jumping Off Rock
when sun peered again to shimmer water far below.
So I was then, as always, in three homes at once:
Forever wherever I am but at Jocassee too,

All the while sitting with the Savior in high heavenly places –
yet more keenly aware of simultaneity on this day when
                      moon
                      sun
                      earth
                                              passed in perfect line
                                              for a few moments in time

Depth Perception Deception

from experience
I finally knew
a kayak moves
the same
over three hundred
feet of water
as over two

so last night
feeling wise,
highly astute,
unlike prior frantic crossings
over this 340-feet-deep pool,
I ceased rowing
to drift

casual, cool
enough to peer
unharried over the side –
but utterly startled to find
I could see, apparently
a regularly ridged sandy beach
down just twenty feet!

perplexed
I checked. My position
told me this could not be
with my kayak over water
deeper than combined height
of three tallest mature white pine trees,
floor black as outer space, no light to see.

glancing
toward heaven, search for an answer,
I leaned back awed underneath
a hundred altocumulus undulatus clouds,
patterned, systematic demarcation lines between –
cleansing breath, pleasant realization I'd been so deceived:
what I'd thought was a floor? a reflected ceiling!

when I
have passed beyond
this world of sight,
what other perceptions will I find
proven so undeniably,
delightfully –
mistaken?

Fear Itself

Pine bark beetles
have gradually
persistently eaten
trees in a circular pattern
on Bully Mountain.
Who knew they chew filigree
tunnels called galleries
inside these trees?
Southern pine beetles
etch away woody flesh
in S shapes;
pine engraver beetles
add H and Y –
finally we see –
their art's secret:
SHY.
Across unharried water
healthy trees stand
on Licklog Mountain
paralyzed
mortified.

A pileated woodpecker
inhabits a hundred-year-old
husky snag of pine.

The only thing we have to fear is fear
misapplied.

In seasons that have
not been utterly dry,
birds still sing
with joy at harvest
of summer fruits.

Most of us
who've lost the skill
the art
the heart
no longer see.
It's what we pay
farmers for –
to notice
to harvest.
And we pay
entertainers
to sing.
Where we live,
only the birds
still fuse
those three things.

Please, don't Round-Up
winged things
who thrive on winged things
in green weeds.
All day kingbirds,
phoebes, and pewees
feast on beetles, flies
and bees.
All light long dragonflies
and damselflies
gobble mosquitoes.

Fear not the forest
as much as the prospect of one last child in the woods.

Yes, danger does live
in these woods:
deep black pools,
dense underbrush,
poison mushrooms,
tripping roots,

slick cliff edge,
copperheads,
black bears,
brown recluse.
Yet which poses
greater lasting danger:
getting lost and dying in a forest
or losing your spirit in closed-in space?
drowning in a mountain lake
or drowning in sedentary malaise
or in a relentless sea
of bills for things you don't need?
poison ivy
or MSG?
Greater likelihood:
black widow bite
or constant high
from fructose corn syrup's
residual, internal swell?

Fear the ones who only fear
fear itself.

His mechanized stationary life
in the buzz of an office cubicle
was not quite intolerable.
Civilized cages kept rattlesnakes away
But he died from venom of road rage
On I-85.

We don't seem to be
afraid of
a lifetime of things
that are not quite fatal
until they are.
We've been warned
Satan will surface
to grab us if we swim

in Devil Hole Falls,
but what if Beelzebub
most likes to hang out
inside
floors and walls?

The worker bees
had taken to staying inside the hive
until management lulled them to lethargy
with toxic smoke screens.
Twenty thousand strong
and ten by ten
they dropped.
The ground, averse, caught them
twitching in the palm of its hand.
Wildflowers bowed their heads dejected.
No one had ever seen a malevolent beekeeper.
No one had ever seen a caterpillar with talons.
No one had ever seen a butterfly with fangs.
That poisonous honey tasted sweeter than ever
until they
every
one
died
even the counterfeit beekeeper himself.

Middle aged, I row out young
at play –
recreating – recreated in the watery breeze.
I speak hello
to two old fishermen
in their john boat,
both glib, indifferent to my mode.
But the face
of the boy with them
shines with curiosity
and longing.

I see his eyebrows raised.
His head turns by degrees
to watch me and my craft
free
until the men
motor him around the bend –
Out of sight.

Fear a strictly inside existence
unaware
of the heart's
groundwater
being fracked.
Fear the weatherman
Who says, "I'm afraid
it's going to be a rainy week."
More than a hoard of wild boar,
fear a Black Friday stampede.

The way the wind stills
at dusk most evenings here
and the water's rippled choppy surface
flattens down smooth as glass –
Fear missing that.
The way great herons fly
with feet curled elegantly back –
Fear missing that.
The way
you would be unable
to see pristine sights
even with perfect eyes
if not for Light –
Fear missing that.

Things Angels Desire to Look Into
shades of vigilance and sense

I know you angels know a thing
or two from what you've seen
long ago of vigilance gone awry.
Despite your mighty airborne guards,
you saw a third of your own kind fall:
you saw luminous eternal beings
led by the most brilliant archangel
expelled, tumbling
with such speed
they made their own tornadic weather
spinning down miles akilter
flapping desperate panicked wing over wing.
Vast
random feathers
loose, cast off
violently
into outer darkness.
I think you still remember
and sometimes it makes you mad as hell.
Sometimes even now you must go to war,
though it makes no sense.
Sometimes you still grieve.

Does it hurt you seraphs how some earthly things
seem senseless?
Have you seen them, owl parents?
They abandon their own fledgling
if they find it's blind.
So in tune with sense of sight,
they refuse to witness
its long futile struggle to survive.
They know hunting vigils
largely depend on eyes
to stay alive.

Have you cherubs watched rescued creatures
through glass pane at wildlife triage?
Like this screech owl – so still – every feather taunt with hurt,
wings and eyes
closed so tightly he's a fraction of his normal size.
But he seems to sense compassionate ones
looking him over intently,
gloved – though scarred – hands turning him
over and over, gently touching
inch by inch from tail tip to ear tuft.
They know one can be deeply wounded
without a trace of blood.
They look to see which threat
caused his distress,
nearly all of human design –
vehicles, firearms, power lines,
barbed wire, clear windows, pesticides.
Do you, like me, ache at him so diminished,
ache and hope he heals to fly?
Do you know underneath the skin
a screech owl's head is mostly eyes?
Large, perceptive, vital eyes.

And I suppose you guardian angels wonder
at some of the humans, fraught with misery,
perpetually edgy, eyes wild and shifty,
caught in prisons of hypervigilance
from underlying tension at nine to surface tension at five,
unwillingly alert to possible trauma that might recur,
on guard for any soul-deep social hurt,
moonlighting fulltime existence as sentinels
on military detail. Maybe they even sense
you watching but mis-see you
as your nemeses waiting on every corner with flaming torches
to transport them on stallions of relentless worry away to hell.

Were you seraphim there to watch
as I tried to rescue a hypervigilant one
from his jail of anxious thoughts?
Bearing a cup of tea, I tapped him on the shoulder,
and he jumped out of his chair, baptizing me
in hot jolt of a startle response.
Shocking! His whole body, electric, twitched.
From where you watched,
did you also get the sense that he was a flight risk?

But I imagine you ethereal ones
who remained fixed in unfallen station
to worship around the throne
marvel at realization
that most anything humanly wounded
can be transformed, healed, reborn, awakened.
I suspect there might be places
like that ladder of Jacob
where you sometimes descend
to witness the victories.

So here – do you see that same one who capsized the tea
who'd been bound in anxiety to such degree
it made no sense to us, to me –
Do you see him now that he is past tense?

I suspect even you angels desire to know:
Is this the same man? The same soul?
I sense you here with us to celebrate
to see him illuminated in that pocket of light breaking
through a section of clouds
as if in his own private sunlit day
(this one for whom night used to last all day)?
Watch him work, loving the earth,
loving this lake, patrolling to notice every detail,
taunt with anticipation, turning his head, eyes owl-wide
from sky to water, water to sky.

Do you bright ones see him paddling towards us across
this place of the lost one, lost in wonder?
Do you see how I've gained a brother?
Do you hear him say
how the leaves have fallen
lilting on lake water,
how they've every one turned
colors gold, frankincense, and myrrh?
How last night he saw a red fox with fur of myrrh?
I know he's found the primitive core.

Do you hear him explain how in his case
such vigilance against potential pain
was transmuted into keen perception
Concentration
Infinite expectation –
by a night when, in final desperation
he finally made his way
outside under the conifers
under an open sky,
how suddenly on his wrist it came to light,
every feather fluffed out wide with life.
How, he'd exclaimed, could it be so tame?
For a soft moment of understanding,
that wing-patched screech owl,
product of saving compassion,
gripped him with gentle talons,
stared him cornea to cornea,
eye to eye.
I see
why
it's something else you desire
to look into, though you've watched it countless times
from your fiery yet unseen posts on the hills.

Turns out it's the Spirit (not the devil) in every detail.

Put Out the Night

"Strange that those who study light always work in the dark" ~ Goethe
"When the morning wakens, / Then may I arise / Pure, and fresh, and sinless / In Thy holy eyes" ~ Sabine Baring-Gould, 1865, hymn "Now the Day is Over"

SOMETIMES, the old swinging
bridge over Whitewater River
appeared in my dreams –
    circadian place
    suspended state –
Sometimes there I could hear
on dusky summer air
voices of Cherokee girls at Ellijay, or
much later, Jocassee Camp girls singing
"Now the Day is Over"….
They sounded untroubled. They sounded free.

    ~ Now, won't someone put out the campfire?
    Young children need their nightly sleep.

THOUGH DARK, it wasn't hard to see.
It wasn't so hard to cross
that foot-worn bridge clinging –
    transitional place
    adventurous state –
steadily holding to the side cable rails.
But I'd wake to find that river erased
under thirty-five quadrillion drops of lake –
Deep. Bolting awake, I'd feverishly wail:
Where's that bridge now?
Where are the guide rails?

Oh yes. I also knew unsettling dreams well.
Sometimes I'd believe I had climbed midway up
Laurel Fork Mountain only to find I was drifting a lake –
> bottomless place
> senseless state –

These mountains couldn't really be climbed anymore.
Flooded-out rivers put us halfway up mountains
just by floating toward Duke Power shores.
Eerie, how getting from the bottom
of any of this valley's mountains to here
now required extra-human scuba gear.

> ~ Won't someone put out the night?
> We're drained from wearing everyday fatigues.

Through the years, I did observe a few with logical tears
who wept over battles for land, over genocide,
and though unjustified, clearly greed was why, unlike –
> the latest comfortless place
> angst-ridden state –

where, increasingly I found absolute tired humankind
weary psychogenesis, universally-traumatized postmodern mind
daunted by mountains of collective, random pain
we could no longer climb.
We used to think of flowers when we heard of Columbine.
We used to breathe open air music waves on Vegas time.

RIGHT. When I strained my ears
for the song of those girls
reaching for some –
> innocent place
> comfortable state –

When I stretched desperate hands
for nature's secure guide rails,

When I rowed out too far,
deceived again there'd be no end to day,
perpetually paddling frantically to beat the dark,
Coley Creek and Wright Falls fading, I'd have to rush away.

> ~ How could we have known we were already in
> the final eight-minute light from extinguished sun?

I'D SEEN seasons recur
when Jocassee turned
a drought-scorched lake –
> dry place
> in-between state –
parched as the wounded
who waited for healing rain,
for an I'm sorry that would never come.
Did I dare speculate
Jocassee still rippled, still pulsated
even while I lay indoors unwaking hours before dawn?

Well, I hope you did.
I certainly speculated like that, my friend,
and found it possible to dream without the blanket of night –
> unfettered place
> in broad daylight state –
That's why I thought it not too late to write
like a Romantic, like a dreamer.
In fact, I came to hold fantasies of flight,
a hope even a wounded culture could suffer a setback sublime,
could undo Keats vilified, harshly criticized.
It shortened his life.

> ~ And in this twilight hour won't someone write
> how nature still carries vestiges of divine light?

There was a time even the night had not
been without love and pleasures,
wonders of stillness in hush of dark –
      exquisite place
      mysterious state –
screech owls, great horned owls, owls striped and barred.
Outside in cool air, we heard them, intermittent,
with frogs and crickets, and we noticed the stars.
We noticed bright winks of a thousand fireflies.
We heard our heartbeats, regular as Marlowe's mighty lines,
regular as lake water lapping the shores of time.

YES, I remember it too, and how delighted I was to find
owls here as well in this new world beyond night,
beyond fear of being prey to those who by stealth survived –
      peaceful place
      perfect state –
Turns out, Lewis rightly theorized
creatures would be here
because treasured in our eyes,
like we were saved by Love of Christ,
yet not just domestic, but prized creatures wild.
The embrace of Love is stunningly wide.

    ~ Though it grew our food and kept us warm,
      that sun was temporary. We do not need it more.

AREN'T you glad, friend, that we'll study war no more?
We love, we feast, but with no death
so we no longer eat the beautiful beasts –
      healed place
      living state –
where we who humbled ourselves to call on Him
find He has healed our nation,

with this new land,
where we night owls hold owls now in our hands,
but they, like us, new creations
fully satisfied beyond the flesh.

Indeed. Like you, I never was a morning person
except on Jocassee days
when I rose early to anticipate –
        hallowed place
        preliminary state –
sun's play on pulsing water
with first light rays.
How fortunate those of us who sensed that heaven
would be like this little Jocassee taste,
yet without any memory of pain, of change,
or loss, or erasure because of its perfect, fully-just Creator.

    ~ Most astounding paradox of history and time:
      He put out the sun's light to put out the night.

So, here we find that eternity
has transformed all true believers
into morning people –
        illuminated place
        elevated state –
How blessed those of us who perceived
the One who orchestrated creation
of such earthly places of awe and amazement
was surely able to elevate us
to a never-ending state of infinite expectation
to a perpetual state of being fully awake.

RIGHT. That was Thoreau's longing,
and though humankind's trip ranged
from Coleridge's fresh thundering streams of Kubla Khan –
     fantastical place
     dreamlike state –
to Eliot's rivers sweating oil and tar
to intuitive Whitewater flooding away her own footbridge years
before the lake could take it
to this final pure river of life pouring from the throne,
everyone in this new earth is Romantic,
lovers of beauty and nature,
both of which are lower case here.

  ~ The One who made light on vast first waters (before
  He even made the sun) will be the Light when the sun is gone.

I USED to wonder how a place
how a state
could be forever new –
     wondrous place
     transcendent state –
I'll admit, sometimes I used to like the dark
and wondered if, when we got here
we'd miss the stars
or if somehow there'd be a different kind
that we could see with transcendent eyes:
could there be any stars if the sky's always light?

But I saw you when you first saw Him,
and I knew you had no question then,
no question when you saw His face –
     brilliant place
     glorious state –
that indeed a star can shine in perpetual day,
The Bright and Morning Star,

ultimate sublime, divine grace.
He's the Upper Case:
Author
and Finisher of our faith.

    ~ Perhaps infinity itself won't give adequate time
       To marvel the sun itself as but temporal shadow
          of His Ideal Light.

In that sense, Plato was right.
Look back at how it went by, time in motion,
Dim torpedo forms shot out in black depth ocean –
    propelled to this place
    ordained state –
And Jocassee too
gave us just a taste
of the deepest beauty
of how water gave life
pointing us to drink Living Water
from Christ.

YES, our thirst was quenched first by His Word,
Then the book of nature was meant to be read,
evidenced by the perfectly illuminated view of space
from where our solar system came to rest.
And the Bard also showed us: tragedies end in death upon death;
comedies end with newlyweds –
    ending place
    completed state –
This new covenant ended with both.
To make it to the church on time, we walked down the aisle
of that shadowed valley into the arms
of the Groom who'd been waiting
in the Light, yet with us all the while.

~ The One who said "Let there be light" had every right
to extinguish the sun and Let there be no more night.

So RAISE the house lights forever,
And give us your hands, friends,
It's the end of our watery play –
    wisest place
    satisfied state –
Let us, these free moral agents,
join all of creation
in bowing to Him:
    We lay down our space of Jocassee days.
    We lay down all we've been blessed to create.
We bow to the One who put out the light to put out the night.
He is the Light. He owns the stage.

~

Notes

~

Introduction

Byron, Lord (George Gordon). *Childe Harold's Pilgrimage, Canto the Fourth. The Longman Anthology of British Literature*. 3rd edition. Vol. 2A. Eds. Susan Wolfson and Peter Manning. New York: Pearson Education, 2006. 724. Print.

Coleridge, Samuel Taylor. "Frost at Midnight." *Longman Anthology*. Eds. Wolfson and Manning. 2006. 577. Print.

Harmless, William. *Mystics*. New York: Oxford UP, 2008.

The Holy Bible, World English Bible Version, public domain. YouVersion Bible App. 2018.

Wordsworth, William. "Lines written a few miles above Tintern Abbey." *Longman Anthology*. Wolfson and Manning. 2006. 405. Print.

Prelude: Double Mind

Ellijay: a town of the Lower Cherokee Nation that was located in the Jocassee Valley. "Ellijay" means green earth, derived from the Cherokee word for mother earth, "Elohi". Thanks to Dr. Dave LaVere for information (on trail trees, Ellijay, Jocassee Town, and burning of the Cherokee stock of corn by Revolutionary War soldiers who destroyed the Native American towns) provided during the lecture on Cherokee History, Lake Jocassee Tour, November 16, 2017 with Jocassee Lake Tours company.

Prelude: Double Mind

Whitewater River: one of four scenic rivers that flow out of steep gorges from North Carolina to join Keowee River and form the lake. The other three rivers include Toxaway River, Thompson River, and Horsepasture River.

red phase: Eastern screech owls have two color phases for feather coloration: a reddish-brown phase and a duller-looking gray phase.

Jocassee Town: a town of the Lower Cherokee Nation that was located right below the confluence of Whitewater and Toxaway Rivers. The sites of both Ellijay and Jocassee Town now lie underneath up to 340 feet of water. Both Ellijay and Jocassee Town were smaller than Keowee Town, just to the south, which was the capital of the Lower Cherokee Nation. The Cherokee controlled 144,000 square miles in an area that is now 8 states (LaVere, Nov. 16, 2017).

trail trees: trees manipulated as saplings by Native Americans who tied them with straps or other materials in order to make them grow in a manner so they pointed to water, trails, or sacred places. Often white oaks or poplars, these trees still can be found standing in various places in the United States and Canada today. Pictures are available online from groups such as MountainStewards.org, who claim to have located 2,034 trail trees across 40 states. https://indiancountrymedianetwork.com/history/geneology/a-groups-quest-to-find-and-save-indian-trail-trees/

Blue Wall: the Cherokee term for the rugged, cliff-filled, blue-hazy Blue Ridge mountains visible to the north of Jocassee Valley, which (positioned at the southern base of the mountains) provides a perfect vantage point for viewing the Blue Wall. Also known as the Blue Ridge Escarpment, "a steep, highly dissected mountain front that marks the change from the mountainous Blue Ridge province to the lower, rolling topography of the foothills zone of the Piedmont province" (online article: "Mountain Topography and Geomorphology," wncvitalityindex.org).

Jocassee's Mine

Attakulla Lodge: a home built in Jocassee Valley by Henry Whitmire, Jr, and later purchased by the Brown family and operated as a hotel on the Whitewater River from the early 1900s to 1951, then afterward a private family residence. After the valley officially began to be flooded in April, 1971, to form the lake, hundreds of feet of water eventually covered the lodge (*Lake Jocassee*, Debbie Fletcher). In 2004, Bill Routh, owner and operator of Lake Jocassee Dive Shop, located the lodge using a remote camera from a boat above, and then a short time later, Routh and other scuba divers were able to descend through over 300 feet to confirm that the lodge (though now lying on its side) was still intact! The story is recorded in the revised edition of *Whippoorwill Farewell: Jocassee Remembered* by Fletcher.

Blue Ridge Escarpment: see Blue Wall on previous page

Mediator

The word "Jocassee" means "Place of the Lost One," and many claim the valley and lake were named from a fictional legend about a young Cherokee woman (often referred to as a "princess") named Jocassee, daughter of Attakullakulla (an important 18th century Cherokee leader, often inaccurately called "Chief Attakulla"). The legend tells that Jocassee fell in love with a member of a rival clan from across the Whitewater River, and that the man she loved was later killed by her own brother in battle, prompting Jocassee to walk about on the water searching for her love's ghost. Though scholars such as Dave LaVere rightly point out that the Cherokee Nation operated as a democracy and therefore had no "princesses," and would not have used the word "chief" at that time, I opted to include this poem as a reference to the possible origins of the place name, and an homage to the grief behind the lake's creation, as well as grief as a universal human occurrence.

Austere Miles

villanelle: a French poetic form with consistent line lengths of 8-10 syllables, using five tercets (groups of 3 lines) all rhyming *aba*, and a quatrain (group of 4 lines), rhyming *abaa*. The entire first and third lines are repeated alternately as the final lines of tercets 2, 3, 4, and 5, and together to conclude the quatrain at the end (definition based on *The Longman Anthology of British Literature*). (The form is notoriously difficult to write).

Tacking

tack: "to change direction of a sailing ship by turning the bow to the wind and shifting sails so as to fall off on the other side at about the same angle as before; to follow a course against the wind by a series of tacks; to follow a zigzag course" (merriam-webster.com). In *Improbable Planet*, Hugh Ross theorizes that Jupiter and Saturn underwent "tacking" motions during the ordering of our solar system prior to the introduction of human life, as part of the process used by the Creator to set up perfect conditions for human life to thrive. Though they and those in their organizations sharply disagree on theories regarding the time-frame for God's creation of all that exists, I appreciate both the work of Hugh Ross and Reasons to Believe, and the work of Ken Hamm and Answers in Genesis. Publications by both organizations provide thought-provoking reading.

Deep

Info on water percentages in the human body ("The water in you," water.usgs.gov).

Deep

trailing clouds of glory do we come: This phrase is from William Wordsworth's ode *Intimations of Immortality* (line 64).

Not Drifting

This poem's content was influenced by the book *Improbable Planet* by Hugh Ross, particularly chapters 3 and 4. Ross theorizes that God's ordering of the just-right conditions for life on Earth did take billions of years. He counters those scientists and others who argue that this long wait was wasted time by claiming that only in a spiral galaxy can life exist for such a long duration as it has on Earth, and that the formation of our spiral galaxy with elements perfect for our existence required a series of complex events including forming, burning, and exploding of giant stars. The cormorant in the poem is not just drifting aimlessly but is instead waiting for the right wind, like the universe was actively waiting, being prepared for perfect conditions for life at just the right time.

May Bees

ontology: "a branch of metaphysics concerned with the nature and relations of being; a particular theory about the nature of being or kinds of things that have existence" (merriam-webster.com)

Silent Spring: influential book published in 1962, written by Rachel Carson to bring awareness about the detrimental effects of pesticides

Cold Comfort

sestina: "a lyrical fixed [poetic] form consisting of six 6-line usually unrhymed stanzas in which the end words of the first stanza recur as end words of the following five stanzas in a successively rotating order". Those same end words appear as "middle and end words" of the lines in the "concluding tercet" (the concluding 3-line stanza) (merriam-webster.com). Sestinas are often written using iambic pentameter (10 syllables per line). For more explanation on how the pattern must go for repetition of the end words, see Sestina at poetryfoundation.org. Though they are one of my favorite poetic forms, I find writing sestinas more challenging even than the villanelle.

lodged: reference to Attakulla Lodge (see the previous note for Jocassee's Mine). Special thanks to Debbie Richardson Fletcher, author and granddaughter of the owner of Attakulla Lodge, who invited me in 2017 to be present onboard a Jocassee dive trip to see talented scuba divers such as Bill Routh of Lake Jocassee Dive Shop and John Baker of Scuba John's Dive Shop begin their descent through 300 feet of water again to explore the lodge at the lake bottom and to bring up treasured relics from her past.

Palindrome Dreams

palindrome: "a word, verse, sentence, or number . . . that reads the same backward or forward" (merriam-webster.com)

The Point

Coriolis effect: "the result of Earth's rotation on weather patterns and ocean currents. The Coriolis effect makes storms swirl clockwise in the Southern hemisphere and counter-clockwise in the Northern hemisphere" (nationalgeographic.org). Although National Geographic writers point out that "the slow rotation of the Earth means the Coriolis effect is not strong enough to be seen in small movements, such as the draining of water in a bathtub," I still use the term in this particular poem for its aesthetic poetic value.

Restitution

The Wall: a large sheer rock wall on the lake (near Jocassee Dam) formed by dynamite blasting during creation of the lake

albatross: refers to the major thematic incident in Samuel Taylor Coleridge's poem *Rime of the Ancient Mariner* in which a sea bird is killed by a sailor for no apparent reason, other than his sin of a careless attitude toward Creation

Reach

Aristotle. *Physics* 194 b 17-20. "Aristotle on Causality." *Stanford Encyclopedia of Philosophy.* 2016. Web. Dec. 2017.

Bad Creek: a pumped-storage hydroelectric facility located on the northwest section of Lake Jocassee in the Whitewater River arm. At times of low energy demand, Duke Power pumps water upward 1,200 feet into Bad Creek reservoir. When electricity demand increases, Duke releases the stored water to rush back down through turbines to generate power. The water is pumped from Jocassee through tunnels in the mountain into the much smaller Bad Creek Reservoir which can be as deep as 300 feet, but because water level can fluctuate as much as 15 feet in an hour, it is closed to any public recreational use. The hydroelectric facility at the other end of Lake Jocassee at the dam is also a pumped-storage facility, pumping water back and forth from Lake Keowee as needed. No doubt these processes are why Kay Wade has called Jocassee "a sacrificial lake" – a lake always giving of herself as her waters are used to meet constant energy demands of modern life (Nov. 16, 2017 tour). (Jocassee Lake Tours is co-owned/operated by Brooks and Kay Wade in Salem, SC).

the one-directional arrow of time: In Chapter 9 of his 1988 book *A Brief History of Time,* Stephen W. Hawking discusses this concept and asks a particularly intriguing question: "Why do we remember the past but not the future?" (144).

Reach

1916 Toxaway River: On Aug. 13, 1916, after an unprecedented amount of rainfall, the Lake Toxaway Dam broke and sent an estimated 5 billion gallons of water shooting at an approximate maximum speed of 55 mph seven miles down the narrow Toxaway River Gorge from North Carolina into the Jocassee Valley, Cane Brake area of South Carolina. Trees, boulders, silt, everything in the path of the water was carried down, scoured to the very bedrock in some long areas still evident. Estimates on amount and speed of water provided on the web by Rick Wooten and personnel of North Carolina Geological Survey, "Geology and Geohazards in Western North Carolina," armarocks.org.

Finding Fault

tectonics: "branch of geology concerned with the structure of the crust of a planet . . . or moon and especially with the formation of folds and faults in it" (merriam-webster.com)

Brevard fault zone: "The most significant fault in the [Carolina] region is the Brevard fault zone, which extends from Alabama to Virginia across North Carolina. . . ." My connection of local earthquakes to the fault zone in the poem is purely imaginative and for thematic purposes since, as scientists point out, "earthquake epicenters in North Carolina [and the Brevard fault zone region] do not consistently line up with known faults" ("Faults and Earthquakes," wncvitalityindex.org)

What's New

sestina: a poetic form - see note for Cold Comfort

Prospero and Miranda: In the final act of Shakespeare's *Tempest*, young Miranda naively exclaims about a group of men who have shipwrecked on their isolated island, "How beauteous mankind is! O brave new world / That has such people in't!" (5.1.185). Her father, Prospero, his perspective previously jaded by the workings of human greed and politics, immediately and glibly responds, "'Tis new to thee" (5.1.186).

Survival Course

rondeau: a poem of 3 stanzas, 13 original lines, plus 2 refrains (words from the first line of the poem repeated at the end of 2nd and 3rd stanzas), usually with 8, sometimes 10 syllables in each line. Typical rhyme scheme of the 3 stanzas: AABBA, AABA, and AABBAA.

Hold Your Fire

heart of darkness: The events described in this poem actually happened. When I witnessed a young man stop his vehicle on the road away from the remote boat ramps, get out, and unload a pistol into the woods, I was reminded of a scene in Joseph Conrad's 1899 novella *Heart of Darkness* in which imperialists set up cannons which they senselessly fire at length into the jungle. There was more to the surreal series of events behind the poem, and I'd be willing to share in greater detail.

Blue Wall Psalms

Blue Wall: the Cherokee term for the rugged, cliff-filled, blue-hazy Blue Ridge mountains visible to the north of Jocassee Valley, which (positioned at the southern base of the mountains) provides a perfect vantage point for viewing the Blue Wall. Also known as the Blue Ridge Escarpment, "a steep, highly dissected mountain front that marks the change from the mountainous Blue Ridge province to the lower, rolling topography of the foothills zone of the

Piedmont province" ("Mountain Topography & Geomorphology," wncvitalityindex.org).

Jocassee Thrust Fault: "a thrust sheet is a large body or package of rock separated from other geologic formations by slip or thrust faults. Thrust nappe is another term for this 'river of rock.' The Jocassee Thrust Sheet [serves as] an excellent example of a generally well-defined, intact thrust sheet" ("Jumping Off Rock," geocaching.com).

Henderson gneiss: very hard, granitic rock of visibly crystalline texture composed partly of quartz, feldspar, and mica ("Southern Appalachian Geology," themareks.com). Details in this poem regarding the colors, composition, and nature of this type of rock were obtained from this site: themareks.com; from the above site: geocaching.com; as well as from definitions of feldspar, mica, gneiss, schist, and quartz from merriamwebster.com

microline: a mineral in feldspar, a shimmery rock

muscovite: colorless to pale brown form of mica, a shiny rock

Google Earth: computer program/app that provides a 3D image of Earth from a bird's eye view, using satellite technology

Cherokee citizens settled near rivers such as those that formerly flowed through Jocassee Valley for a number of reasons, including their belief that a river was absolutely necessary "to constitute a paradise" (Dr. Dave LaVere, Jocassee Lake Tours, lecture, Nov. 16, 2017).

The line about joy in the Whitewater River psalm section of this poem was inspired by Hannah Hurnard who says in her book *Mountains of Spices*, "joy is sorrow overcome and transformed" (68). This is a prominent theme in many of Hurnard's works, including *Hinds' Feet on High Places*.

Wild Honey

James Moore: Some believe that in 1690, Moore "led a British expedition through the area [now known as Jocassee] in search of gold" (jocassee.com/jocassee_history).

Hernando de Soto: While some claim that this Spanish explorer came through the area in 1539 (jocassee.com/ jocassee_history), others such as Dave LaVere hold that evidence for the visit is slim (lecture, Nov. 16, 2017).

Andre Michaux: French botanist, one of the first white visitors recorded to have come to what is now known as the Jocassee Valley, Jocassee Gorges area to collect specimens in 1787-88. Kay Wade of Jocassee Lake Tours notes that Michaux described the thundering sound of Whitewater Falls, the terribly cold nights, snow, wind, thunderstorms preceding strong cold fronts (lake tour, Nov. 16, 2017). While on his visit to the Cherokee country, Michaux encountered a rare plant known as shortia galacifolia, commonly called the Oconee bell, a wildflower with small white blooms, native primarily to just a few counties in this area of Appalachia.

kabbalah: originated in mainstream Judaism but came to refer to a set of beliefs including the idea that only a select few are granted secret knowledge from God in order to truly understand the hidden wisdom of scripture

alchemy: efforts originating in the Middle Ages which sought the ability to turn "base metals into gold, the discovery of a universal cure for disease, and the discovery of a means of indefinitely prolonging life" (merriam-webster.com)

philosopher's stone: the imaginary base substance that alchemists sought and saw as the key to all of their alchemical efforts; also referred to as the elixir of life or first matter, it was believed to be the originating substance of which everything else is derived. The belief was that if one could produce this material, one would have the secret to solve all of the problems of human existence and to achieve all wealth, perfection, and immortality.

Jocassee's Green Bird

uweyv: Cherokee word for river

Oconee was a Cherokee town on the main British/Cherokee trading path between Charleston and the Mississippi River. In 1868, the South Carolina county in the Jocassee location was named Oconee, which is derived from the Cherokee word "Aequonee" meaning land beside the water. Others, though, have claimed the word Oconee comes from the word "Ukoona," which means **watery eyes of the hills.**

We n' de ya ho: called the "Cherokee Morning Song" in English, the history of the song is disputed. Some claim that the song, popularized by the modern singing trio Walela, is not actually native Cherokee but was adopted from other Native American nations or nomadic groups over the years by many Cherokees. One source writes, "It was sung by women only as part of the morning prayers, facing the rising sun, welcoming the new day. The men sang a different song that could be blended or even done as a 'round' with the women's song" (speakcherokee.blogspot.com). Others claim that the song is, in fact, an ancient Cherokee song (lyricsmode.com). If that was the case, then it would be possible for the song to have been sung in that time period (as sung here by the fictional Jocassee), though there is no evidence available to support the claim. The language of the Lower Cherokee clans that lived in SC is now extinct. Either way, the song has *become* a Cherokee song today, sung and often translated as "I am of the Great Spirit" (though the song's phrase does not appear in Cherokee dictionaries).

Jocassee's Green Bird

Carolina parakeet: now extinct, the only parrot species native to the Eastern US, the birds with their "colorful feathers (green body, yellow head, and red around the bill)," lived in old-growth forests on rivers ("The last Carolina parakeet," johnjames audubon.org). "The species probably fled North Carolina by the 1780s but may have lingered in South Carolina until the 1860s" ("Carolina Parakeet," ncpedia.org). The last one is thought to have died in captivity at Cincinnati Zoo in 1918.

Eastatoee: According to a fictional legend for which many claim the valley and the lake were named, the Oconee tribe of Jocassee (known as the Brown Vipers) lived on the west side of the Whitewater River, and the Eastatoee tribe (known as the Green Birds) of Nagoochie (the man Jocassee loved, who was killed by her brother in a battle) lived on the east side of the Whitewater River, in an area known today as Eastatoe. Some believe this was the spot of the last sighting of a Carolina parakeet in SC.

Cosmic Storm

Charybdis: "a whirlpool off the coast of Sicily personified in Greek mythology as a female monster" (merriam-webster.com)

Scylla: "a nymph changed into a monster in Greek mythology who terrorizes mariners in the Strait of Messina" (merriam-webster.com)

***Paradise Lost*, Book IV:** In *Paradise Lost,* a poem published in 1674 about how Satan came to tempt Adam and Eve to disobey God in the Garden of Eden, John Milton creatively imagines how events surrounding those outlined in scripture might have gone. The passage I referenced from the poem's Book IV is typical of the thought-provoking, entertaining nature of Milton's work. At the end of Book IV (which takes place prior to the actual temptation of

Eve by Satan in the garden), Milton imagines Satan has been caught (lurking around Eden and even whispering to Eve while she sleeps) by 2 angels sent by Gabriel to guard Adam and Eve. The 2 angels capture Satan and bring him before Gabriel. When Gabriel asks Satan why he is again rebelling against God, an intensely heated exchange of words and insults takes place between Satan and Gabriel. For example, when Gabriel tells Satan that if he doesn't leave Eden, he'll take him back to hell in chains, Satan replies in a rage with a personal attack on Gabriel (put in modern language here): well, isn't this an appropriate response from one who knows chains very well since you are used to being in bondage to God? The other angels turn fiery red in response and move in on Satan with their spears. They are on the verge of a violent war in Eden, and Gabriel states that he would like to trample Satan like mud, but – prompted by a sign from God, Gabriel lets Satan go. Satan flees, murmuring, which indicates that this conflict is far from over.

Wright Creek Bluegrass

This poem was inspired by the well-known quote, "Paddle faster: I hear banjo music!". I have been unable to identify the author of the quote, but it appears frequently on t-shirts in the Jocassee area. The idea no doubt was inspired by the 1972 film *Deliverance* starring Burt Reynolds and Jon Voight which featured scenes filmed at Jocassee, including the actual moving of a graveyard and a church from the valley as the lake was being created. Unfortunately, the film's authors depicted local banjo-playing residents as depraved, sadistic criminals. To reverse this perception, I was inspired to write this poem. Appalachian banjo pickers are some of the finest people I know, and if I heard banjo music echoing over Jocassee, I would certainly paddle faster – toward the music, not away from it.

Wright Creek: On the northwest side of Jocassee, this creek comes down the mountain to form Wright Creek Falls, a span of 3 separate cascades, the lowest of which spills into the lake.

Wright Creek Bluegrass

Gold Tone: a brand of banjo which features a series of several different resonator banjos called Cripple Creek

Cripple Creek: Appalachian folk tune by an unknown composer; a standard frequently performed by bluegrass musicians on banjo and fiddle

drone: On a five-string banjo, this shorter fifth string can be tuned to a higher open pitch than the other four full-length strings. Other relevant definitions for drone include "to make a sustained deep murmuring, humming, or buzzing sound" and the musical definition "an instrument or part of an instrument . . . that sounds a continuous unvarying tone" (merriamwebster.com). Banjo players use the thumb on the drone string for this purpose and to add melody notes.

float with ghosts behind the strings: When the lake is at full pond, one can pull a boat directly up to Wright Creek Falls or kayak behind the falls. When lake levels are down, one can walk behind the falls.

Shine

a certain slant of light: from a line by Emily Dickinson

Abbot Suger: Elected Abbot of the French monastery, the Abbey of St. Denis, Suger was in charge of renovating the church around 1140. Influenced by the views of Dionysius that "the material world was no hindrance to spirituality . . . but was, if seen rightly, aglow with divine presence, a shimmering gateway back to God" (*Mystics*, Harmless, 98), Suger took advantage of a recent invention – stained glass – and had large stained glass windows inserted into the church for the first time. His "renovations became the template for every cathedral in France" and thus influenced many thinkers and writers to meditate on how the beauty of color and light can lead us to an understanding of the beauty of God.

Shine

St. Francis of Assisi: Founder of the Franciscan Order and Italian Catholic known for his care for the sick and the poor, and his special love and care for animals. In 1220, he was reported to have seen a large flock of birds and to have approached them and preached a sermon to them about how and why they should live in thankfulness to God. Witnesses claimed that the birds, which had been loudly chirping before, stopped all noise and listened to Francis in stillness. The text of the brief sermon is available online: ("Sermon to the Birds," historyplace.com).

Testify!

For details in sections of the poem on creatures and conditions in frigid places and desert environments, I consulted 2 issues of *National Geographic:* the article on "Secret Antarctica" (July 2017), and many of the articles on cold and hot realms in the special Nat Geo edition called *50 of the World's Last Great Places* (2012). The Jocassee Gorges area was featured in this 2012 publication as one of these 50 last great places. However, details in the Jocassee section of my poem come almost entirely from animals, plants, and sights that I have personally observed on or near the lake during many expeditions there.

Jumping Off Rock

Jumping Off Rock: a cliff formation above the northeast corner of the lake which offers a view of the water, valley, and surrounding mountains that many (myself included) hail as the most spectacular sight in the state of SC

Double Springs Harmonic

Perpetuum Mobile: piece of classical music by Ottokar Novacek in which I think the violin might be the closest musical parallel to the call of a screech owl

Bassoon Concerto in B-Flat Major, K. 191: II. Andante ma adagio: piece of classical music by Wolfgang Amadeus Mozart in which I think the bassoon sounds similar to the call of a barred owl

Taps: played on a bugle at military bases and locations, Taps "signals that unauthorized lights are to be extinguished. This is the last call of the day. The call is also sounded at the completion of a military funeral ceremony" (music.army.mil). The hauntingly solemn-sounding call of loons might be compared with the stirring sound of Taps, in addition to the timing parallel – loons call at dusk to close the day.

Whistling: A Handbook

Ephraim: historical name, central mountainous district of Israel

Anna Leonowens: depicted in the Rodgers and Hammerstein musical *The King and I*, Anna's character performs the song "I Whistle a Happy Tune" in which she describes how whistling dispels her fears – and does a bit of whistling in the course of the song.

transitional object: psychological term for an object often used by children to help them cope with natural separation from a parent or with fears in general; also known as comfort object, security blanket

Mother of All Theories

theory of everything: For several centuries, physicists have sought a single, unified theory that would explain all the workings of the universe in one – a theory of what makes the universe operate and what holds it all together. Such a theory remains elusive in the realm of science. One major field of exploration focuses on gravity, while another major field focuses on non-gravitational forces such as microscopic particles, molecules, atoms.

Ducks in a Row

row: this term refers to several different concepts in the poem. "Row" can mean an orderly straight line of things, or to move a watercraft using paddles or oars, but the word has another meaning relevant to this poem: "Row" can also mean an uproar, quarrel, or loud disturbance (and that form of the word is actually pronounced to rhyme with "Now" rather than "Glow").

the course of true love never did run smooth: a line from Shakespeare's *A Midsummer Night's Dream*

Trilocation

Bilocation: "the state of being or ability to be in two places at the same time" (merriamwebster.com). **Trilocation** is a word I created to reflect being in three places at once.

St. Isidore: St Isidore the Farmer of Madrid, Spain, also called St. Isidore the Laborer, was known for his devotion to prayer, church, hard work, the poor, and like St. Francis, compassionate treatment of animals. Many believe that Isidore had the capability of bilocation, for there were stories such as the one in which some witnessed him plowing the field while others simultaneously saw him fervently praying in church.

Depth Perception Deception

altocumulus undulatus clouds: cloud formations that tend to appear as long strips of grey or white, giving the look of undulations like waves of water. Their dramatic undulating separations are caused by wind shear or abrupt changes in wind direction or speed. To see photos, search the term in Google Images.

Fear Itself

one last child in the woods: a reference to Richard Louv's 2005 book *Last Child in the Woods: Saving Our Children from Nature-Deficit Disorder*

Things Angels Desire to Look Into

hypervigilance: a hypervigilant person or animal experiences an ongoing heightened state of nervous arousal stemming from trauma and is constantly alert to threats of repeated trauma

Jocassee: the word means Place of the Lost One

primitive core: psychological concept explored by Freud, Jung, and others

Put Out the Night

Baring-Gould, Sabine. "Now the Day is Over." *Church Times.* London, 1865. Public Domain. Web. Hymnary.org. Dec. 2017.

Goethe, Johann Wolfgang. Quoted in *What is Light?* by ACS van Heel and CHF Velzel. New York: McGraw-Hill, 1968. 13. Print.

Put Out the Night

Special font emphasis: There are three different speakers in **Put Out the Night**: one speaks stanzas beginning with all caps; one speaks stanzas beginning with italics; and one speaks two-line stanzas beginning with the ~ symbol.

Jocassee Camp: Camp Jocassee for Girls was developed at what previously had been the Whitewater Inn on the Whitewater River in Jocassee Valley. The camp operated from 1921 to 1970 when the property was acquired and flooded to create the lake.

Keats vilified: Literary reviews of the Romantics' poetry were often harsh. Particularly personal and negative reviews of his poem *Endymion* left Keats, who was already suffering from ill health, dejected. His fellow poet Percy Shelley believed that the review actually contributed to shortening Keats's life.

Marlowe's mighty line: Playwright Christopher Marlowe, a contemporary of William Shakespeare, used the blank verse form (with iambic pentameter lines of 10 syllables each) in such an innovative, influential way that Ben Jonson, also a noted playwright of the time, called the form "Marlowe's mighty line".

Lewis rightly theorized: In Chapter 9 of *The Problem of Pain*, C.S. Lewis theorizes that animals with whom we have had relationships (such as pets we have deeply loved and cared for) will gain immortality and be reunited with us after death. The idea is that like Christians will go to heaven because they are "in Christ," the animals will go because they are "in us" – in our spirits because of the redeeming spiritual and unconditional love we had for them. Lewis also speculates that some wild animals might be in the afterlife, particularly those that symbolize aspects of God in meaningful ways, such as lions. I would argue, however, that each type of wild animal that has ever existed can be viewed as symbolizing at least one aspect of God's character or abilities – so, if animals are to be preserved in the afterlife based on that criterion, then perhaps representatives of each type will be there.

Put Out the Night

Revelation 21:23-25: "And the city had no need of the sun, neither of the moon, to shine in it: for the glory of God did lighten it, and the Lamb is the light thereof. And the nations of them which are saved shall walk in the light of it. . . . And the gates of it shall not be shut at all by day: for there shall be no night there." See also Rev. 22:5.

Thoreau's longing: "To be awake is to be alive. I have never met a man who was quite awake. How could I have looked him in the face? We must learn to reawaken and to keep ourselves awake, not by mechanical aids, but by an infinite expectation of the dawn, which does not forsake us in our soundest sleep" (*Walden*).

Kubla Khan: Samuel Taylor Coleridge's poem depicting streams of pure water crashing through deep mysteriously intriguing gorges

Eliot's rivers sweating tar and oil: In his poem *The Wasteland*, the most influential early poem of the Modern Literary Period, T.S. Eliot depicts rivers as stagnant, turbid, and highly polluted.

Plato: In his "Allegory of the Cave," Greek philosopher Plato depicts the human condition using the image of people chained to the wall inside a dark cave where they can only look at shadows on the wall, unable to see the real forms on the other side of a fire which cast the shadows.

Book of Nature: a belief that began in the Middle Ages that in addition to sacred scripture, nature was a book in which we can see and read truths God reveals about himself

perfectly illuminated view of space: In *Improbable Planet,* Hugh Ross states, "The solar system's move to a safer location for advanced life also happened to carry it to the best imaginable site for a view to the wonders of the universe" (41).

the Bard: William Shakespeare

April Phillips Boone holds an MA in English (Renaissance Literature) from Western Carolina University and a PhD in British Literature from The University of Tennessee at Knoxville. She taught writing and literature for 17 years, most recently as Assistant Professor of English at North Greenville University in South Carolina. She lives in the mountains of Western North Carolina with her husband Kevin, who is a minister. Boone wrote her doctoral dissertation on Edmund Spenser's sixteenth-century poem called *The Faerie Queene*, and often finds (in Spenserian fashion) that her research leads her to an interdisciplinary place: She loves to see ideas from diverse fields and traditions come together, when possible. In addition to writing, researching, studying nature, and kayaking, April enjoys painting, playing guitar, and singing. She appreciates music from all genres, but is most passionate about worship music and sings the praises of Christ at every opportunity.

To send comments or to schedule a poetry reading, contact the author on her Facebook page, **April Phillips Boone, Author** or via her blog at **https://aprilphillipsboone.wordpress.com**

www.ingramcontent.com/pod-product-compliance
Lightning Source LLC
Chambersburg PA
CBHW022132080426
42734CB00006B/331